ANGULAR INTE[illegible] QUESTIONS AND ANSWERS

INCLUDING ANGULAR 6,5, 4 AND 2

ANIL SINGH

FIRST EDITION 2018

ISBN: 9789388176699

LIMITS OF LIABILITY AND DISCLAIMER OF WARRANTY

Distributors:

BPB PUBLICATIONS
20, Ansari Road, Darya Ganj
New Delhi-110002
Ph: 23254990/23254991

BPB BOOK CENTRE
376 Old Lajpat Rai Market,
Delhi-110006
Ph: 23861747

DECCAN AGENCIES
4-3-329, Bank Street,
Hyderabad-500195
Ph: 24756967/24756400

MICRO MEDIA
Shop No. 5, Mahendra Chambers, 150
DN Rd. Next to Capital Cinema, V.T.
(C.S.T.) Station, MUMBAI-400 001 Ph:
22078296/22078297

Published by Manish Jain for BPB Publications, 20, Ansari Road, Darya Ganj, New Delhi-110002 and Printed by Repro India Ltd., Mumbai

Table of Contents

Preface

Changing job is one of the biggest challenges for any IT professional. When IT professional starts searching job, they realise that they need much more than experience. Working on a project is one thing and cracking an interview is another. This book will give you a bird's eye view of what is needed in an interview. It will help you in doing a quick revision so that you can be ready for the discussion faster.

Acknowledgements

I would like to thank my parents, wife, and daughter who patiently supported me in writing this book.

Thank you so much to my publisher (BPB), readers and reviewers for their feedbacks.

Chapter 1
The Basic Concepts of Angular

1.1 What is Angular?

Angular is a most popular web development framework for developing mobile apps and desktop applications.

Angular framework is also utilized in the cross-platform mobile development called IONIC and is not limited to web apps only.

Angular is an **open source framework** written and maintained by Angular team at Google and the Father of Angular is Misko Hevery.

Misko Hevery - Agile Coach at Google, Attended Santa Clara University and Lives in Saratoga, CA.

Angular is written in TypeScript and it comes with all the capabilities that typescript offers.

The core concepts of Angular:

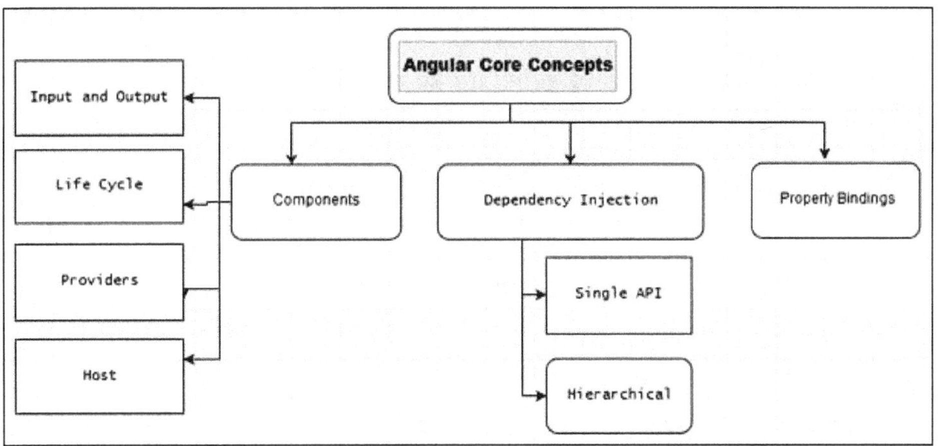

You don't worry about the TypeScript versions. The compiler manages to the versioning related problems and Angular team working with Traceur compiler team to provide the support to build some extensions.

Angular's current target release dates and versions:

Date	Stable	Compatibility
September/October 2018	7.0.0	^6.0.0
March/April 2019	8.0.0	^7.0.0

1.2 What are Angular Prerequisites?

Before you can install Angular 4 or higher versions, you must need to have some prerequisites.

You must have **Node.js** installed.

You must have **NPM** (Node Package Manager) installed.

```
node -v
```

Noted Points:

We need to setup our machine's local environments which are:

1. node.js >= 6.9.x
2. npm >= 3.x.x
3. Visual Studio Code or Atom

You can download the installer-*https://nodejs.org/en/download/*

1.3 What is Angular CLI?

The Angular CLI (Command Line Interface) is a tool to initialize, develop, scaffold and maintain Angular applications.

OR

The Angular CLI (Command Line Interface) is a set of tools that are used to initialize, develop, generate files, scaffold, and test & maintain Angular application.

You can use CLI commands to generate an app, the default AppModule is as follows –

```
ng new yourApp
```

The above CLI command is used to create a new Angular project and this CLI command will automatically creates several folders and files which are necessary for project development, testing, configuration and so on.

To use Angular CLI, we need to install it first (globally on your machine).

```
npm install -g @angular/cli
```

1.4 How to Update Angular CLI?

If you're using Angular CLI lesser version, uninstall an angular-cli package and install new versions of CLI.

```
npm uninstall -g angular-cli
npm uninstall —save-dev angular-cli
```

Global package:

```
npm uninstall -g @angular/cli
npm cache clean
npm install -g @angular/cli@latest
```

Local project package:

```
rm -rf node_modules dist # use rmdir /S/Q node_modules dist
in Windows Command Prompt; use rm -r -fo node_modules,dist
in Windows PowerShell
npm install —save-dev @angular/cli@latest
npm install
```

Some Additional CLI Commands:

1. ng new
2. ng serve
3. ng generate
4. ng lint
5. ng test
6. ng e2e
7. ng build
8. ng get
9. ng set
10. ng doc
11. ng eject
12. ng xi18n
13. and many more

1.5 What's New in Angular 2?

What are the differences between AngularJs and Angular 2?

Angular 2 is a TypeScript based open-source front-end web application platform led by the Angular Team at Google and by a community of individuals and corporations. Angular 2 is a complete rewrite from the same team that built AngularJs.

Angular 2 is a platform that makes it easy to build applications with the web. Angular 2 combines declarative templates, dependency injection, an end to end tooling, and integrated best practices to solve development challenges. Angular empowers developers to build applications that live on the web, mobile, or the desktop.

The first version of AngularJs was released in the year 2010 while Angular 2 was released in the year 2016.

Both AngularJs and Angular 2 are completely different. Actually, Angular 2 is entirely component based and AngularJs is both scope and controller based.

Angular 2 is a platform and framework for building client applications in HTML and TypeScript. Angular 2 is written in TypeScript. It implements core and optional functionality as a set of TypeScript libraries that you import into your apps.

Angular 2 is used on Cross-platform, modern browsers only. The core differences and many more advantages on Angular 2 vs. AngularJs are:

1. Angular 2 is entirely component based, while AngularJs is controllers and scope based.
2. Angular 2 has better change detection as compare to AngularJs.
3. Angular 2 has better performance as compare to AngularJs.
4. Angular 2 has a more powerful template system.
5. Angular 2 provide simpler APIs, lazy loading and easier to application debugging.
6. Angular 2 is much more testable.
7. Angular 2 provides nested level components. Ahead of Time compilation (AOT) improves rendering speed.
8. Angular 2 execute run more than two programs at the same time. The Angular 2 structural directives syntax is changed like ng-repeat is replaced with *ngFor etc.
9. In Angular 2, local variables are defined by using prefix (#) hash. You can see the below *ngFor loop Example. TypeScript can be used for developing Angular 2 applications.
10. Better syntax and application structure. There are more advantages over performance, template system, application debugging, testing, components, and nested level components.

For Examples as:

AngularJs Controller:

```
var app = angular.module("userApp", []);
app.controller("productController", function($scope) {
   $scope.users = [{ name: "Anil Singh", Age:35, department
:"IT"},
        { name: "Aradhya Singh", Age:5, department :"MGMT"
},
        { name: "Reena Singh", Age:28, department :"HR" }];
});
```

Angular 2 Components using TypeScript:

Here the @Component annotation is used to add the metadata to the class.

import {Component } from 'angular2/core';

```
@Component({
  selector: 'usersdata',
  template: '<h3>{{users.name}}</h3>'
})
export class UsersComponent {
```

```
  users = [{ name: "Anil Singh", Age:35, department :"IT"},
        { name: "Aradhya Singh", Age:5, department :"MGMT"
},
        { name: "Reena Singh", Age:28, department :"HR" }];
}
```

Bootstrapping in AngularJs using ng-app :

```
angular.element(document).ready(function() {
  angular.bootstrap(document, ['userApp']);
});

Bootstrapping in Angular 2 :
import { bootstrap } from 'angular2/platform/browser';
import { UsersComponent } from './product.component';
bootstrap(UserComponent);
```

The Angular 2 structural directives syntax is changed like ng-repeat is replaced with *ngFor and so many.

For example as:

```
//AngularJs
<div ng-repeat="user in users">
   Name: {{user.name}}
   Age : {{user.Age}}
   Dept: {{user.Department}}
</div>
```

And

```
//Angular 2,
<div *ngFor="let user of users">
     Name: {{user.name}}
     Age : {{user.Age}}
     Dept:  {{user.Department}}
</div>
```

1.6 What's New in Angular 4?

What are the differences between Angular 2 and Angular 4?

Off-course! Angular 4 being smaller, faster, easier to use and it will be making developer's life easier as compare to Angular 2.

Angular 2 is released in the year 2016 whereas Angular 4 is released in the year 2017.

Angular 2 and Angular 4 will use the same concept and patterns.

Angular 4 contains some additional enhancement and improvement.

Consider the following enhancements:

1. Smaller & Faster Apps.
2. View Engine Size Reduce.
3. Animation Package.
4. NgIf and ngFor Improvement.
5. Template.
6. NgIf with Else.
7. Use of AS keyword.
8. Pipes.
9. HTTP Request Simplified.
10. Apps Testing Simplified.
11. Introduce Meta Tags.
12. Added some Forms Validators Attributes.
13. Added Compare Select Options.
14. Enhancement in Router.
15. Added Optional Parameter.
16. Improvement Internationalization.

- **Smaller & Faster Apps** - Angular 4 applications is so smaller and faster in comparison with Angular 2.
- **View Engine Size Reduce** - Some changes under to hood to what AOT generated code compilation that means in Angular 4, improved the compilation time. These changes reduce around 60% size in most cases.
- **Animation Package**- Animations now have their own package i.e. @angular/platform-browser/animations
- **Improvement** - Some Improvement on *ngIf and *ngFor.
- **Template** - The template is now *ng-template*. You should use the "ng-template" tag instead of "template". Now Angular has its own template tag that is called "ng-template".
- **NgIf with Else** – Now in Angular 4, possible to use an else syntax as,

```
<div *ngIf="user.length > 0; else empty"><h2>Users</h2></
div>
```

And

```
<ng-template #empty><h2>No users.</h2></ng-template>
```

- **AS keyword** – A new addition to the template syntax is the "as keyword" is used to simplify to the "let" syntax.

Use of as keyword,

```
<div *ngFor="let user of users | slice:0:2 as total; index as
= i">
  {{i+1}}/{{total.length}}: {{user.name}}
</div>
```

To subscribe only once to a pipe "|" with "async" and If a user is observable, you can now use to write,

```
<div *ngIf="users | async as usersModel">
   <h2>{{ usersModel.name }}</h2> <small>{{ usersModel.age
}}</small>
</div>
```

- **Pipes** - Angular 4 introduced a new "titlecase" pipe "|" and use to changes the first letter of each word into the uppercase.

The example as,

```
<h2>{{ 'anil singh' | titlecase }}</h2>
<!— OUPPUT - It will display 'Anil Singh' —>
```

- **Http** - Adding search parameters to an "HTTP request" has been simplified as,

```
//Angular 4 -
http.get('${baseUrl}/api/users', { params: { sort: 'ascending'
} });
```

And

```
//Angular 2-
const params = new URLSearchParams();
params.append('sort', 'ascending');
http.get('${baseUrl}/api/users', { search: params });
```

- **Test**- Angular 4, overriding a template in a test has also been simplified as,

```
//Angular 4 -
TestBed.overrideTemplate(UsersComponent, '<h2>{{users.name}}</
h2>');
```

And

```
//Angular 2 -
TestBed.overrideComponent(UsersComponent, {
    set: { template: '<h2>{{users.name}}</h2>' }
});
```

- **Service**- A new service has been introduced to easily get or update "Meta Tags" i.e.

```
@Component({
  selector: 'users-app',
  template: '<h1>Users</h1>'
})
export class UsersAppComponent {
  constructor(meta: Meta) {
      meta.addTag({ name: 'Blogger', content: 'Anil Singh'
});
  }
}
```

- **Forms Validators** - One new validator joins the existing "required", "minLength", "maxLength" and "pattern". An email helps you to validate that the input is a valid email.
- **Compare Select Options** - A new "compareWith" directive has been added and it used to help you to compare options from a select.

```
<select [compareWith]="byUId" [(ngModel)]="selectedUsers">
      <option *ngFor="let user of users"
[ngValue]="user.UId">{{user.name}}</option>
</select>
```

- **Router** - A new interface "paramMap" and "queryParamMap" has been added and it is introduced to represent the parameters of a URL.

```
const uid = this.route.snapshot.paramMap.get('UId');
this.userService.get(uid).subscribe(user => this.name = name);
```

- **CanDeactivate** - This "CanDeactivate" interface now has an extra (optional) parameter and it is containing the next state.
- **I18n** - The internationalization is tiny improvement.

```
//Angular 4-
<div [ngPlural]="value">
      <ng-template ngPluralCase="0">there is nothing</ng-
template>
   <ng-template ngPluralCase="1">there is one</ng-template>
</div>
```

And

```
//Angular 2-
<div [ngPlural]="value">
      <ng-template ngPluralCase="=0">there is nothing</ng-
template>
   <ng-template ngPluralCase="=1">there is one</ng-template>
</div>
```

1.7 What's New in Angular 5?

What is the difference between Angular 4 and Angular 5?

Off-course! Angular 5 being smaller, faster, easier to use and it will be making developer's life easier as compare to Angular 2.

Angular 4 is released in the year 2017 while Angular 5 is released on 1st November 2017.

Angular 5 is going to be a much better Angular and you will be able to take advantage of it much easier.

Angular 5 contains a bunch of new features, performance improvements and a lot of bug fixes and also some surprises to Angular lovers:

1. Smaller and Faster Apps.
2. Build optimizer - It helps to removed unnecessary code from your application.
3. Angular Universal State Transfer API and DOM Support.
4. Supports TypeScript 2.3+ version.
5. Compiler Improvements - It makes AOT the default and *ng serve/s –aot.*
6. Increased the standardization across all browsers.
7. Watch mode.
8. Type checking in templates.
9. More flexible metadata.
10. Remove *.ngfactory.ts files.
11. Better error messages.
12. Smooth upgrades.
13. Tree-Shakeable components.
14. Hybrid Upgrade Application.
15. Include Representation of Placeholders to xliff and xmb in the compiler.
16. Include an Options Arg to Abstract Controls in the controls of the form.
17. Include add default updateOn values for groups and arrays to form controls.
18. Include updateOn blur option to form controls.
19. Include updateOn submit option to form controls.
20. Include an Events Tracking Activation of Individual Routes.
21. Include NgTemplateOutlet API as stable in the common controls.
22. Create StaticInjector which does not depend on Reflect polyfill.
23. Include [@.disabled] attribute to disable animation children in the animations.

- **HttpClient** - Earlier In Angular 5, we were using @angular/HTTP module for all HTTP requests but in Angular 5 *@angular/http* module has been deprecated and introduced new *HttpClientModule* module and imports from *@angular/common/http* package.

The HttpClient communicate with backend services over the HTTP protocol and the Improvements is:

1. Improvement on Type-checking the response.
2. Improvement on Reading the full response.
3. Improvement on Error handling and fetching error details.
4. Improvement in Intercepting all requests or responses.
5. Improvement on Logging.
6. Improvement on Caching.
7. Improvement on XSRF Protection.

The Angular team recommends using HttpClientModule.

Angular 5 Added new router lifecycle events for Guards and Resolvers:

1. GuardsCheckStart,
2. GuardsCheckEnd,
3. ResolveStart and
4. ResolveEnd

Some Bug Fixes in Angular 5:

1. Fixed compilation error by using the correct type for providers.
2. Skip PWA test when redeploying non-public commit.
3. Don't strip CSS source maps. This is the compiler related fix.
4. Remove tsickle (language-service) dependency.
5. Support persisting dynamic styles within animation states.
6. Ignore @import in multi-line CSS.
7. Fix platform-browser-dynamic.
8. Forbid destroyed views to be inserted or moved in VC.
9. Support persisting dynamic styles within animation states.

1.8 What's New in Angular 6?

What is the difference between Angular 5 and Angular 6?

Off-course! Angular 6 being smaller, faster, easier to use and it will be making developer's life easier.

The **Angular Team** are working on lots of bug fixes, new features to be added/ update/remove/ re-introduce/ and many more things.

Let's start to explore all the changes of Angular 6 step by step!

- **Added ng update** - This CLI commands will update your angular project dependencies to their latest versions. The ng update is normal package manager tools to identify and update other dependencies.

```
ng update
```

- **Angular 6 uses RxJS 6** - this is the third-party library (RxJS) and introduces two important changes as compared to RxJS 5.

1. RxJS 6 introduces a new internal package structure.
2. Operator concept.

Both require you to update your existing code.

To update to RxJS 6, you simply run:

```
npm install —save rxjs@6
```

Simply run the below command and update your existing Angular project:

```
npm install —save rxjs-compat
```

Alternatively, you can use the command - *ng update rxjs* to update *RxJS* and install the *rxjs-compat* package automatically.

RxJS 6 Related import paths:

Instead of:

```
import { Observable } from 'rxjs/Observable';
import { Subject } from 'rxjs/Subject';
```

Use a single import:

```
import { Observable, Subject } from 'rxjs';
```

So all from *rxjs/Something* imports become from one *'rxjs'*

Operator imports have to change:

Instead of:

```
import 'rxjs/add/operator/map';
import 'rxjs/add/operator/throttle';
```

Now you can use:

```
import { map, throttle } from 'rxjs/operators';
```

And

Instead of:

```
import 'rxjs/add/observable/of';
```

Now you can use:

```
import { of } from 'rxjs';
```

RxJS 6 Changes - Changed Operator Usage -

Instead of:

```
import 'rxjs/add/operator/map';
import 'rxjs/add/operator/throttle';
yourObservable.map(data => data * 2)
.throttle(...)
.subscribe(...);
```

You can use the new pipe () method:

```
import { map, throttle } from 'rxjs/operators';
yourObservable
  .pipe(map(data => data * 2), throttle(...))
  .subscribe(...);
```

- **ICLI update and added a new project config file** - Instead of ".angular-cli.json" use "angular.json"

Now in Angular 6 new projects use "angular.json" file instead of ".angular-cli.json" file.

```
ng update @angular/cli –from=1 –migrate-only
```

The above command will help you to update your existing ".angular-cli.json" file to the new "angular.json" file.

The "angular.json" file contains the Properties:

1. **Version:** This is integer file format version and it is currently 1.
2. **newProjectRoot:** This is string path where new projects will be created.
3. **defaultProject:** This is default project name used in commands.
4. **CLI:** This is workspace configuration options for Angular CLI and it contains:
   - defaultCollection.
   - packageManager.
   - Warnings.
   - And so on.
5. **Schematics:** This is configuration options for Schematics.
6. **Projects:** This is configuration options for each project in the workspace and it contains:
   - root.
   - sourceRoot.
   - projectType.
   - prefix.
   - Schematics.
   - ***Architect:*** This is the project configuration for Architect targets.

- **The <template> deprecated, Now Angular 6 introduce <ng-template>:** Now in Angular 6, you should use *<ng-template>* instead of *<template>*

For example, previously you are using

```
<template [ngIf]="IsAdmin">
  <p>This template renders only if IsAdmin is true.</p>
</template>
```

Now in Angular 6, you should use <ng-template> instead of <template>

```
<ng-template [ngIf]="IsAdmin">
  <p>This template renders only if IsAdmin is true.</p>
</ng-template>
```

- **Service level changes (the way of marking a service as global):** In the earlier versions, if you want to provide a service to the entire application –you should add it to *providers []* in the AppModule but in the Angular 6 released you should not add in the *providers []* in the AppModule.

Example for marking a service as global:

Instead of

```
//my.service.ts
export class MyService { }
//In app.module.ts
//JavaScript imports services
import { MyService } from './my-serice.service';

//AppModule class with the @NgModule decorator
@NgModule({
  declarations: [],
   providers: [MyService] //My services instances are now
available across the entire app.
})
export class AppModule {
   //exporting app module
}
```

Use with Angular 6 released-

```
//my.service.ts
@Injectable({providedIn: 'root'})
export class MyService { }
@NgModule({
  declarations: [],
  providers: [] // Service does not need to be added here
})
export class AppModule {}
```

The second one obviously saves some lines of code as compared to the previous code.

Angular 6 introduces Angular Elements

The elements are a feature that allows you to compile Angular components to native web components which you can use in your Angular application.

An angular element is a package which is part of the Angular framework @angular/elements.

Angular 6 introduces new Ivy Renderer

The new Ivy renders and it's not stable for now and it's only in beta version. It will stable in future for production.

The main goal of Ivy render is to speed up its loading time and reduce the bundle size of your applications. Also for uses a different approach for rendering Angular components.

Ivy Renderer is new rendering engine which is designed to be backward compatible with existing render and focused to improve the speed of rendering and it optimizes the size of the final package.

For Angular, this will not be default renderer, but you can manually enable it in compiler options.

Bazel Compiler

The Bazel Complier is a build system used for nearly all software built at Google.

From Angular 6 release, will start using the Bazel compiler support and when you compile the code with Bazel Compiler, you will recompile the entire code base, but it compiles only with necessary code.

The Bazel Complier uses advanced local and distributed caching, optimized dependency analysis and parallel execution.

Replace Context, Record, and Injectors:

Replace ngOutletContext with ngTemplateOutletContext

Replace CollectionChangeRecord with IterableChangeRecord

Now use Renderer2, Instead of Renderer

Now use StaticInjector, Instead of ReflectiveInjector

Angular 6 Renamed Operators

The lists of renamed operators are:

- do() => tap()
- catch() => catchError()
- finally() => finalize()
- switch() => switchAll()
- throw() => throwError()
- fromPromise() => from()

Angular 6 introduces multiple validators for array method of FormBuilder:

```
import { Component } from '@angular/core';
import {FormsModule, FormBuilder, FormGroup} from '@angular/
forms';
constructor(private fb: FormBuilder) {}
myForm: FormGroup;
ngOnInit() {
  this.myForm = this.fb.group({
      text: ['', Validators.required],
        options: this.fb.array([], [MyValidators.minCount,
MyValidators.maxCount])
  });
}
```

- **Addition of navigationSource and restoredState to NavigationStart:** These two properties help us to handle the multiple use cases in routing.
- **NgModelChange:** Now emitted after value and validity is updated on its control. Previously, it was emitted before updated. As the updated value of the control is available, the handler will become more powerful.

Previously -

```
<input [(ngModel)]="name" (ngModelChange)="onChange($event)">
```

And

```
onChange(value) {
  console.log(value);   // would log the updated value, not
old value
}
```

Now Use:

```
<input #modelDir="ngModel" [(ngModel)]="name"
(ngModelChange)="onChange(modelDir)">
```

And

```
onChange(NgModel: NgModel) {
   console.log(NgModel.value);// would log old value, not
updated value
}
```

- **Form Control statusChanges:** Angular 6 emits an event of "PENDING" when we call Abstract Control markAsPending.
- **New optional generic type ElementRef:** This optional generic type will help to get the hold of the native element of given custom Element as ElementRef Type.

Let's see in depths:

1. Typescript 2.7+ supports.
2. Added Angular Material and CDK Stable.
3. Component Dev Kit (CDK) - CDK allows you to build your own library of UI components using Angular Material.
4. Improved decorator error messages.
5. Fix platform-detection example for Universal.
6. Ivy Renderer - It is a new backward compatible and main focused area - speed improvements, size reduction, and increased flexibility.
7. Add afterContentInit and afterContentChecked to render.
8. Added to supports of nativeElement.
9. Added Optional generic type for ElementRef.

   The Example looks like:

```
@ViewChild('your-element') yourElement:ElementRef;
```

10. **Bazel Compiler:** Bazel only rebuilds what is necessary.
11. Added Test Comment.
12. Add missing lifecycle tests for projected components.
13. **Closure Compiler:** Closure Compiler consistently generates smaller bundles.
14. Rename QueryPredicate to LQuery and LQuery to LQueries.
15. **Service Worker:** Service worker is a script that runs in the web browser. It also manages to cache for an application.
16. Added multiple validators for array method of FormBuilder.
17. **Handle string with and without line boundary:** Now Handle string with and without line boundary (^ & $) on pattern validators. Previously, it works with string, not boundaries.
18. **AbstractControl statusChanges:** Previous version, not emits an event when you called "markAsPending" but now emits an event of "PENDING" when we call AbstractControl markAsPending.
19. **Updates on NgModelChange:** Now emitted after value and validity is updated on its control. Previously, it was emitted before updated.
20. Allow HttpInterceptors to inject HttpClient:

    Previously, an interceptor attempting to inject HttpClient directly would receive a circular dependency error, as HttpClient was constructed via a factory which injected the interceptor instances. Users want to inject HttpClient into interceptors to make support.

    Either HttpClient or the user has to deal especially with the circular Dependency. This change moves that responsibility into HttpClient itself.

    By utilizing a new class HttpInterceptingHandler which lazily Loads the set of interceptors at request time, it's possible to inject HttpClient directly into interceptors as a construction of HttpClient no longer requires the interceptor chain to be constructed.

21. Add navigationSource and restoredState to NavigationStart – Currently, NavigationStart there is no way to know if navigation was triggered imperatively or via the location change.

    These two use cases should be handled differently for a variety of use cases (e.g., scroll position restoration). This PR adds a navigation source field and restored navigation id (passed to navigations triggered by a URL change).
22. Add type and hooks to directive def.
23. Enable size tracking of a minimal CLI render3 application.
24. Add canonical view query.
25. **Language Service:** The 2.6 version of Typescript's "resolveModuleName" started to require paths passed to be separated by '/' instead of being able to handle '\'.

Where to download the Angular 6?

For download Angular 6, kindly refer below link.

https://github.com/angular/angular/releases/

1.9 What's New in Angular 7?

What's New In Angular 7?

Angular 7 being smaller, faster and easier to use and it will be making developers life easier.

Angular 7 is a major release and expanding to the entire platform including core framework, Angular Material, and Angular CLI (stands for Command Line Interface).

Let's introduce added new features of Angular 7 -

1. Added a new compiler –Angular Compatibility Compiler (ngcc)
2. Added a new interface - UrlSegment interface
3. Added a new interface - DoBootstrap interface
4. Introduce a new Pipe called - KeyValuePipe
5. Now supporting to TypeScript 2.9 and higher.
6. Added a new elements features - enable Shadow DOM v1 and slots
7. Added a new router features - warn if navigation triggered outside Angular zone
8. Added a new mapping for ngfactory and ngsummary files to their module names in AOT summary resolver.

9. Added a new “original” placeholder value on extracted XMB
10. Added a new ability to recover from malformed URLs
11. Added a new Drag & Drop feature
12. Added a new compiler support dot (.) in import statements and also avoid a crash in ngc-wrapped
13. Update compiler to flatten nested template fns

Angular Compatibility Compiler (NGCC)

The Angular Compatibility Compiler (ngcc) is a tool which “upgrades” node_module compiled with non-ivy ngc into ivy compliant format.

This compiler will convert node_modules compiled with ngcc, into node_modules which appear to have been compiled with TSC compiler transformer (ngtsc) and these compiler conversions will allow such “legacy” packages to be used by the Ivy rendering engine.

TSC transformer which removes and converts @Pipe, @Component, @Directive and @NgModule to the corresponding definePipe, defineComponent, defineDirective and defineInjector.

Ivy rendering engine -

The Ivy rendering engine is a new backwards-compatible Angular renderer main focused on the following.

1. Speed Improvements
2. Size Reduction
3. Increased Flexibility

The template functions for creating dynamically views are no longer nested functions inside each other.

Now we use for loops that are nested inside other loops.

Example:

```
functionAppComponent(rf: RenderFlags, ctx: AppComponent) {
functionulTemplateFun(rf1: RenderFlags, ctx0: any) {
functionliTemplateFun(rf1: RenderFlags, ctx1: any) {...}
  }
}
```

No longer create multiple functions instances for loops that are nested inside other loops.

Example:

```
<ul *ngFor="let student of students">
<li *ngFor="let subject of student"> {{subject}} </li>
</ul>
```

To enabling Ivy by adding the following lines to the tsconfig.json file in the new project folder:

```
"angularCompilerOptions": {
"enableIvy": true
}
```

UrlSegment interface

The UrlSegment interface represents a single URL segment and the constructor, properties, and methods look like below UrlSegment class i.e.

```
classUrlSegment {
constructor(path: string, parameters: {...})
path: string
parameters: {...}
toString(): string
}
```

The UrlSegment is a part of a URL between the two slashes and it contains a path and matrix parameters associated with the segment.

Example:

```
@Component({
templateUrl:'./user.component.html',
styleUrls: ['./user.component.css']
})
classUserComponent {
constructor(router: Router) {
consturlTree: UrlTree = router.parseUrl('/user;id=101');
consturlSGroup:          UrlSegmentGroup          =
urlTree.root.children[PRIMARY_OUTLET];
consturlSegment: UrlSegment[] = urlSGroup.segments;

urlSegment[0].path; // It will returns 'user'
urlSegment[0].parameters; //It will returns {id: 101}
  }
}
```

DoBootstrap interface

Angular 7 added a new lifecycle hook that is called ngDoBootstrap and an interface that is called DoBootstrap.

Example:

```
//ngDoBootstrap - Life-Cycle Hook Interface
classAppModuleimplementsDoBootstrap {
ngDoBootstrap(appRef: ApplicationRef) {
appRef.bootstrap(AppComponent);
  }
}
```

KeyValuePipe

Chang, you object into an array of key-value pairs that output array will be ordered by keys.

By default, it will be by Unicode point value.

Syntax:

```
{{your_input_expression | keyvalue [:compareFn] }}
```

Example:

```
@Component({
selector:'key-value-pipe',
template:'<div>
<p>your custom Object</p>
<div *ngFor="let cust of customerObject | keyvalue">
      {{cust.key}}:{{cust.value}}
</div>
</div>'
})
exportclassKeyValuePipeComponent {
customerObject: {[key: number]: string} =
   {
      1:'Anil Singh',
      2:'Aradhaya Singh',
      3:'Reena Singh'
   };
 }
```

1.10 What is Bootstrapping (bootstrap) in Angular?

The Bootstrap is the root AppComponent that Angular creates and inserts into the "index.html" host web page.

```
<body>
  <app-root></app-root>
</body>
```

You can put more than one component tree on a host web page, that's not typical. Most of the applications have only one component tree and they bootstrap a single root component and you can call the one root component you want but most developers call it AppComponent.

The bootstrapping process creates the components listed in the bootstrap array and inserts each one into the browser (DOM).

The Angular Module (NgModules) helps us to organize an application into connected blocks of functionality.

The NgModule properties for the minimum "AppModule" generated by the CLI which follows as:

- **Declarations** — Use to declare the application components.
- **Imports** — every application must import BrowserModule to run the app in a browser.
- **Providers** — there are none to start.
- **Bootstrap** — this is a root AppComponent that Angular creates and inserts into the index.html host web page.

app.module.ts -

```
import { BrowserModule } from '@angular/platform-browser';
import { NgModule } from '@angular/core';

import { AppComponent } from './app.component';
import { LoginComponent } from './login/login.component';
import { SignupComponent } from './signup/signup.component';

@NgModule({
  //declarations is used for configure the selectors.
  declarations: [
    AppComponent,
    LoginComponent,
    SignupComponent
  ],
  //Composability and Grouping
  //imports used for composing NgModules together.
  imports: [
    BrowserModule
  ],
  //Runtime or injector configuration
  //providers is used for runtime injector configuration.
  providers: [],
```

```
  bootstrap: [AppComponent]
})
export class AppModule { }
```

By default Bootstrap file is created in the folder "src/main.ts" and "main.ts" file is very stable. Once you have set it up, you may never change it again and its looks like -

```
import { enableProdMode } from '@angular/core';
import { platformBrowserDynamic } from '@angular/platform-browser-dynamic';
import { AppModule } from './app/app.module';
import { environment } from './environments/environment';

if (environment.production) {
  enableProdMode();
}

platformBrowserDynamic().bootstrapModule(AppModule)
  .catch(err => console.log(err));
```

1.11 What Is Architecture Overview of Angular?

Angular is a most popular web development framework for developing mobile apps as well as desktop applications.

The Angular framework is also utilized in the cross-platform mobile development called *IONIC* and so it is not limited to web apps only.

Angular is an open source framework written and maintained by Angular team at *Google* and the Father of Angular is *Misko Hevery*.

The bootstrapping process creates the components listed in the bootstrap array and inserts each one into the browser (DOM).

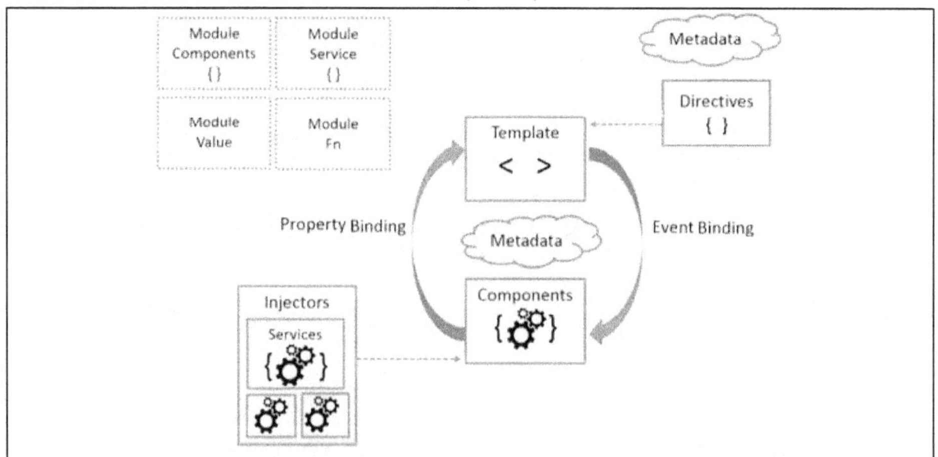

With bits of the help of above pic, you can identify the seven main building blocks of an Angular Application, which are:

1. Component
2. Templates
3. Metadata
4. Data Binding
5. Directives
6. Services
7. Dependency Injection

The basic building blocks of an Angular application are NgModules, which provide a compilation context for components.

Angular app is defined by a set of NgModules and it always has at least a root module that enables bootstrapping, and many more feature modules.

1. Components define views
2. Components use services

Introduction to Modules

The NgModule is a class and work with the @NgModule decorator function and also takes a metadata object that tells Angular how to compile and run module code.

The purpose of the module is to declare everything you create in Angular and group them together.

The NgModule is used to simplify the ways you define and manage the dependencies in your applications and also you can consolidate different components and services into associative blocks of functionality.

Introduction to Components

Components are the most basic building block of a UI in Angular applications and it controls views (HTML/CSS). They also communicate with other components and services to bring functionality to your applications.

Introduction to Templates

The Template is just a subset of HTML, which tells Angular how to display the HTML view. Templates are created by using the normal HTML tags and also use the Angular-specific markup like interpolation or Property binding.

1. Interpolation – {{}} double-curly braces
2. Property binding – []

Most of all HTML syntax is valid template syntax.

A template expression produces a value. Angular executes the expression and assigns it to a property of a binding target. The target might be HTML elements, components, or directives.

The <script> element is a notable exception. It is forbidden, eliminating the risk of script injection attacks.

In practice, <script> is ignored and a warning appears in the browser console.

The *<html>, <body>, and <base>* elements have no useful role.

```
Interpolation double-curly braces - {{…}}
```

You met the double curly braces of interpolation, {{and}}, early in your Angular education.

```
<p>Welcome you, {{user.name}}</p>
```

Introduction to NgModule metadata

The @NgModule takes a metadata object that tells Angular how to compile and launch the application.

- **Data binding:** Angular uses Data Binding to get the data from the Component to Template View with the help of Template Syntax.

Angular supports four types Data binding

1. **Interpolation:** It used to bind the data from component to View.
2. **Property Binding:** It used to bind the data from component to the property of an HTML control in the view
3. **Event Binding:** The DOM Events are bind from View to a Component method.

- **Pipes** – "Pipes transform displayed values within a template."

Use the @Pipe annotation to declare that a given class is a pipe. A pipe class must also implement a PipeTransform interface.

The @Pipe decorator allows you to define the pipe name that is globally available for use in any template in the across Angular apps.

Pipe decorator and metadata –

```
@Pipe({
  name: string
  pure?: boolean
})
```

The pipe name is used for template bindings.

- **Directives:** Angular Directive is a TypeScript class which is declared as the @directive decorator.

  The directives allow you to attach behavior to DOM elements and the @directive decorator provide you an additional metadata that determines how directives should be processed, instantiated, and used at run-time.

- **Services:** Services are commonly used for storing data and making HTTP calls.

  The main idea behind a service is to provide an easy way to share the data between the components and by the bits of the help of dependency injection (DI) you can control how the service instances are shared.
- **Dependency injection:** Dependency Injection is a powerful pattern for managing code dependencies. DI is a way to create objects that depend upon other objects.

  Angular has its own DI framework pattern, and you really can't build an Angular application without Dependency injection (DI).
- **Routing:** Together, a component and template define an app view.

1.12 What are the differences between Interpolations vs. Property Binding?

- **Data Binding:** The Data binding helps you to communicate between a component and template for rendering the views.

  Two type of Data Binding:
  1. One-ways
  2. Two-ways
  - ***One-Way Data-Binding:*** The one-way data binding flows a value in one direction from a component's data property into a target element property.
  - ***Two-Way Data-Binding:*** The Two-way bindings synchronize the data between the model and the view.

The Two-way data binding means that any data-related changes affecting the model are immediately propagated to the matching views, and that any changes made in the views are immediately reflected in the underlying model.

The example looks like:

Interpolation:

```
import { Component } from '@angular/core';

@Component({
    selector: 'auther-app',
    template: '<h1>{{ authorName }}</h1>
  <img src='{{authorPic}}' style="height:40px"/>'
})
export class AuthorComponent {
    authorName: string = 'My Name is - Anil Singh';
      authorPic: string = 'https://code-sample.com/images/
author/anil_singh.png'
}
```

- **Property Binding:** The target property in the following code is the image element's src property.

```
import { Component } from '@angular/core';

@Component({
    selector: 'auther-app',
    template: '<h1 [innerHtml]='authorName'></h1>
    <img [src]='authorPic' style="height:40px"/>   '
})
export class AuthorComponent {
    authorName: string = 'My Name is - Anil Singh';
     authorPic: string = 'https://code-sample.com/images/
author/anil_singh.png'
}
```

Some people prefer the bind- prefix alternative, known as the canonical form -

```
import { Component } from '@angular/core';

@Component({
    selector: 'auther-app',
    template: '<h1 [innerHtml]='authorName'></h1>
    <img bind-src='authorPic' style="height:40px"/>   '
})
export class AuthorComponent {
    authorName: string = 'My Name is - Anil Singh';
     authorPic: string = 'https://code-sample.com/images/
author/anil_singh.png'
}
```

The target name is always the name of a property, even when it appears to be the name of something else.

Angular data binding sanitizes the values before displaying on DOM. It will never allow HTML or script tags to leak the security into the browsers. It will never alert for dangerous HTML, script tags and render the content harmlessly.

Both Interpolation and Property Binding sanitize the malicious content.

Attribute, class, and style bindings

- **Attribute binding:** This binding start with the attr prefix, its followed by a dot (.), and the name of the attribute.

The example looks like -

```
<table border=0>
  <!— The below expression calculates colspan = 2 —>
  <tr><td [attr.colspan]="1 + 1">Gender</td></tr>

  <!— GOT ERROR, If TRY BELOW LINE OF CODE AND ERROR IS -
There is no 'colspan' property to set!
    <tr><td colspan="{{1 + 1}}">Gender</td></tr>
  —>
  <tr><td>M</td><td>F</td></tr>
</table>
```

- **Class binding:** You can add and remove element's CSS classes with the help of class binding.

The example looks like:

```
<div class="row" [class.row]="!IsActive">This one is not
active row!</div>
```

- **Style binding:** This binding start with style prefix, followed by a dot (.), and the name of a CSS style property

The example looks like -

```
<button [style.color]="IsActive ? 'red': 'dark'">This is a
red!</button>
```

And

```
<button [style.font-size.%]="!IsActive ? 50 : 100" >This is
not active!</button>
```

- **Remember points:** To set an element property to a non-string data value, you must use property binding.

Otherwise Angular go through the process of converting your interpolation to property binding. So it will not good for your apps.

1.13 What Is the class Decorator?

Without using a class decorator, AppComponent is just a class. There is nothing Angular about it. It is the decorator, which tells angular how to treat the class.

Angular currently has 7 class decorators -

1. @Component
2. @Directive
3. @Injectible

4. @NgModule
5. @Pipe

1.14 What are Observables?

Observables help you to manage asynchronous data and asynchronous event handling.

Observables are lazy and it can have multiple values over time. Observable is an interface and use to handle asynchronous operations.

The HTTP Client module uses observables to handle the AJAX requests and responses.

1. Angular HttpClient returns observables from HTTP method calls.
2. The EventEmitter class extends Observable.
3. The Router modules use observables to listen and respond to user events.
4. The Forms modules use observables to listen and respond to user events.

To use observables, Angular uses a third-party library called Reactive Extensions (RxJS).

1.15 What Is Lifecycle hook?

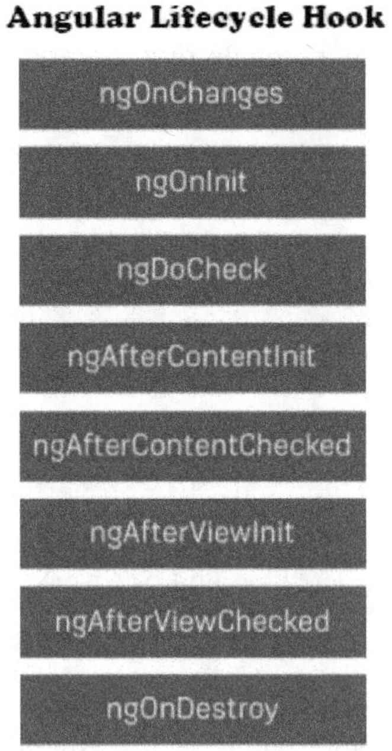

Angular Lifecycle Hook

ngOnChanges
ngOnInit
ngDoCheck
ngAfterContentInit
ngAfterContentChecked
ngAfterViewInit
ngAfterViewChecked
ngOnDestroy

Angular offers eight hooks to allow you to tap into the lifecycle of directives and components as they are created, updated, and destroyed.

Each has a single hook method with the name prefixed ng.

Angular calls these hook methods in the following order:

1. ngOnChanges – Called after input and output binding value changes.
2. ngOnInit - Called once the components is initialized.
3. ngDoCheck - Called during every change detection.
4. ngAfterContentInit - Called after component content initialized.
5. ngAfterContentChecked - Called after every check of component content.
6. ngAfterViewInit - Called after a component's and child's views has been initialized.
7. ngAfterViewChecked - Called every time the component's and child's views has been checked.
8. ngOnDestroy - Called just before the directive is destroyed.

The ngOnInit() and ngOnDestroy() methods play the important roles in the real applications.

Use of ngOnInit()

There are two main reasons to Use ngOnInit method i.e.

1. The ngOnInit method is used to perform the complex initializations shortly after construction.
2. The ngOnInit method is used to set up the component after Angular sets the input properties.

Use of OnDestroy()

The OnDestroy method is used to clean-up logic and it must run before Angular destroys the directive.

If you neglect to call the destroy method that you may risk on memory leaks.

1.16 What is Modular View Engine Architecture?

Angular View Engine could be implemented, such as:

1. Taking a multi-threaded approach to rendering.
2. Generating Web-Assembly code.
3. Generating SPIR-V code to exploit the work of the important W3C gpuweb working group.
4. Generating Verilog for a FPGA.
5. Deeper integration with native platforms.

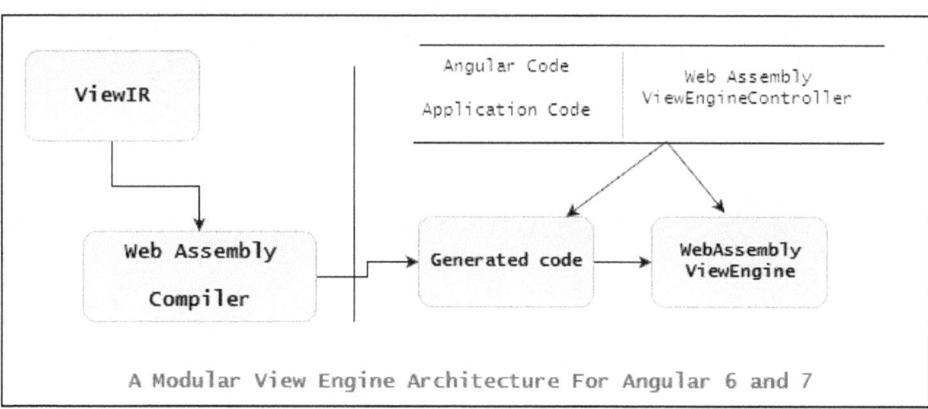

A Modular View Engine Architecture For Angular 6 and 7

There are three possible approaches to built on Angular 6 and 7 to facilitate "modular view engines" and it can:

1. do nothing
2. do a little
3. do a lot

- **Do Nothing:** No changes are needed to be carried out to the existing Angular 6 code.

- **Do a Little:** Making small changes to Compiler CLI so that the shared functionality between the different view compilers can be defined once.
- **Do a Lot:** Realizing that supporting multiple view engines is going to be important in the future and investing now the necessary engineering effort to structure on-going development.

Chapter 2
Angular Components

2.1 What Are Components in Angular?

Components are the basic building block of UI in Angular applications and it controls the views (HTML/CSS). They also communicate with other components and services to bring functionality to your applications.

Technically components are basically TypeScript classes that interact with the HTML files of the components, which get displayed on the browsers.

The component is the core functionality of Angular applications but you need to know to pass the data into the components to configure them.

Angular applications must have a root component that contains all other components.

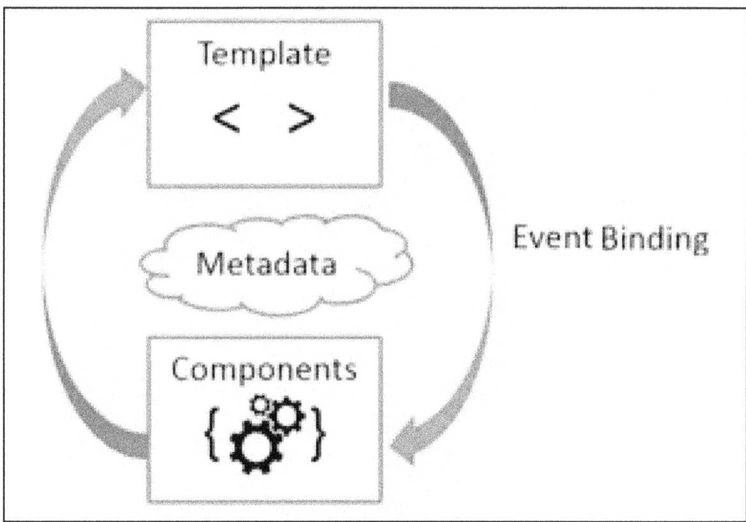

Components are created by using **@Component** decorator that is a part of **@angular/core module**.

You can create your own project by using Angular CLI, this command will allows you to quickly create an Angular application like - generate components, services, pipes, directive, classes, and modules, and so on as per your requirements.

Create your own component (login) using below command line –

```
ng g component login
```

After executing the above Angular CLI command in your project directory, the result looks like –

```
D:\Angular\DemoApp>ng g component login
  create src/app/login/login.component.html (24 bytes)
  create src/app/login/login.component.spec.ts (621 bytes)
  create src/app/login/login.component.ts (265 bytes)
  create src/app/login/login.component.css (0 bytes)
  update src/app/app.module.ts (394 bytes)
```

And the application login files are created by default and it looks like –

1. login.component.html
2. login.component.spec.ts
3. login.component.ts
4. login.component.css
5. app.module.ts

And Angular CLI commands also import the Login component in the Angular module.

See the example in details:

login.component.ts:

```
import { Component, OnInit } from '@angular/core';

@Component({
  selector: 'app-login',
  templateUrl: './login.component.html',
  styleUrls: ['./login.component.css']
})
export class LoginComponent implements OnInit {

  constructor() { }

  ngOnInit() {
  }
}
```

The above component class shows some of the most useful **@Component** configuration options:

1. Selector
2. TemplateUrl
3. Style URLs

- **The selector** – It is a CSS selector that tells Angular to create an instance of this component wherever it finds the corresponding tag in template HTML. For example, it is - <app-login></app-login>

- **The templateUrl** – It is the module-relative address of this component's HTML template and you can also provide the inline HTML template.
- **The style Urls** - It can be used for CSS rules and it will affect the style of the template elements and you can also provide the inline style CSS.

The components provide you some additional metadata configurations–

```
@Component({
  changeDetection?: ChangeDetectionStrategy
  viewProviders?: Provider[]
  moduleId?: string
  templateUrl?: string
  template?: string
  styleUrls?: string[]
  styles?: string[]
  animations?: any[]
  encapsulation?: ViewEncapsulation
  interpolation?: [string, string]
  entryComponents?: Array<Type<any> | any[]>
  preserveWhitespaces?: boolean
  // inherited from core/Directive
  selector?: string
  inputs?: string[]
  outputs?: string[]
  host?: {...}
  providers?: Provider[]
  exportAs?: string
  queries?: {...}
})
```

app.module.ts –

```
import { BrowserModule } from '@angular/platform-browser';
import { NgModule } from '@angular/core';
import { AppComponent } from './app.component';
import { LoginComponent } from './login/login.component';

@NgModule({
  declarations: [
    AppComponent,
    LoginComponent
  ],
  imports: [
    BrowserModule
  ],
  providers: [],
```

```
  bootstrap: [AppComponent]
})
export class AppModule { }
```

login.component.html –

```
<p>
  Welcome you, Anil!
</p>
```

login.component.spec.ts –

```
import { TestBed, async } from '@angular/core/testing';
import { AppComponent } from './app.component';
describe('AppComponent', () => {
  beforeEach(async(() => {
    TestBed.configureTestingModule({
      declarations: [
        AppComponent
      ],
    }).compileComponents();
  }));

  it('should create the app', async(() => {
    const fixture = TestBed.createComponent(AppComponent);
    const app = fixture.debugElement.componentInstance;
    expect(app).toBeTruthy();
  }));

  it('should have as title 'app'', async(() => {
    const fixture = TestBed.createComponent(AppComponent);
    const app = fixture.debugElement.componentInstance;
    expect(app.title).toEqual('app');
  }));

  it('should render title in a h1 tag', async(() => {
    const fixture = TestBed.createComponent(AppComponent);
    fixture.detectChanges();
    const compiled = fixture.debugElement.nativeElement;
   expect(compiled.querySelector('h1').textContent).toContain('Welcome
to app!');
  }));
});
```

The detail about Component's Metadata Properties List:

1. **Selector Property:** The CSS selector that identifies this component in a template.
2. **StyleUrls Property:** The list of URLs to style sheets to be applied to this component's view.
3. **Styles Property:** To be applied the inline styles for the component's view.
4. **Template Property:** To be applied the inline template for the component's view.
5. **TemplateUrl Property:** Used the URLs to an external file containing a template for the view.
6. **Animations Property:** Applied the list of animations of this component.
7. **ChangeDetection Property:** The change detection strategy used by this component.
8. **Encapsulation Property:** The style encapsulation strategy used by this component.
9. **EntryComponents Property:** Used the list of components that are dynamically inserted into the view of this component.
10. **ExportAs Property:** The name under which component instance is exported in a template.
11. **Host Property:** Used to map the class property to host element bindings for events, properties, and attributes.
12. **Inputs Property:** The list of class property names to data-bind as component inputs.
13. **Interpolation Property:** The custom interpolation markers used in this component's template.
14. **ModuleId Property:** This is the CommonJS module id of the file in which this component is defined.
15. **Outputs Property:** The list of class property names that expose output events that others can subscribe too.
16. **Providers Property:** The list of providers available to this component and its children.
17. **Queries Property:** To configure queries that can be injected into the components.
18. **ViewProviders Property:** The list of providers available to this component and its view children.

Summary:

Components are the fundamental building blocks of UI in Angular applications and it communicates with other components and services to bring functionality to your applications.

1. It is a core component of Angular applications.
2. An angular application must have a root component that contains all other components.
3. They have well-defined selector.
4. They have well-defined styles and style Urls.
5. They have well-defined template and templateUrl.
6. They have well-defined inputs and outputs.
7. They have well-defined encapsulation and animations.
8. They have a well-defined lifecycle.
9. They are self-describing property.

2.2 What Is an Entry Component?

The entry component is used to define components and created dynamically by using the ComponentFactoryResolver.

Firstly, Angular creates a component factory for each of the bootstrap components with the help of ComponentFactoryResolver. And then, at runtime, it will use the factories to instantiate the components.

You specify an entry component by bootstrapping in the Angular module or you specify an entry component by routing definition.

Entry components are not tied to routes. They are loaded dynamically and are not referenced in component templates.

All other root components should be listed in the declarations array.

```
const routes: Routes = [
    { path: '', redirectTo: 'home', pathMatch: 'full'},
    { path: 'login', component: LoginComponent },
    { path: 'dashboard', component: DasboardComponent },
    { path: '**', redirectTo: 'home' }
];
```

There are two main kinds of entry components which are following:

1. The bootstrapped root component
2. A component you specify in a route

The bootstrapped entry component

A bootstrapped component is an entry component that Angular loads into DOM at the application launch and the other root components loaded dynamically into entry components.

The angular loads a root dynamically because it is bootstrapped in the Angular Module. In the below example, AppComponent is a root component so that angular loads dynamically.

The following is an example of specifying a bootstrapped component -

```
import { BrowserModule } from '@angular/platform-browser';
import { NgModule } from '@angular/core';
import { AppComponent } from './app.component';
import { LoginComponent } from './login/login.component';
@NgModule({
  declarations: [
    AppComponent,
    LoginComponent
  ],
  imports: [
    BrowserModule
  ],
  providers: [],
  bootstrap: [AppComponent] // bootstrapped entry component
})
export class AppModule { }
```

A Routed entry component

All router components must be entry components because the component would require you to add in two places.

1. Router and
2. EntryComponents

The Angular compiler is so smarter and it is recognizing that this is a router component and it automatically adds router components into entry components.

A route definition refers to components by its type i.e.

1. LoginComponent
2. DasboardComponent

There are two components one is Login and another one is Dashboard. These components have the ability to navigate between the login and dashboard views if passed the authentication and authorization of this app.

Example -

```
const routes: Routes = [
    { path: '', redirectTo: 'home', pathMatch: 'full'},
    { path: 'login', component: LoginComponent },
    { path: 'dashboard ', component: DasboardComponent },
    { path: '**', redirectTo: 'home' }
];
```

2.3 Why does Angular need entry components?

The entry components improve the performance, smallest, fastest and reusable code of your production apps.

For example, if you want to load the smallest, fastest and reusable code in your production apps. These codes contain only the classes that you actually need and it should exclude the components that are never used, whether or not those components are declared in the apps.

As you know, many libraries declare and export components you will never use in your app. If you do not reference them, the tree shaker drops these libraries and components from the final code package.

The following is an example of specifying a bootstrapped component:

```
@NgModule({
  declarations: [
    AppComponent
  ],
  imports: [BrowserModule],
  providers: [],
 bootstrap: [AppComponent]  // bootstrapped entry component
})
export class AppModule { }
```

If a component is not in an entry component, the compiler skips compiling for this component.

2.4 What's the difference between a Bootstrap Component and an Entry Component?

A bootstrapped component is an entry component that Angular loads into DOM at the application launch and the other root components loaded dynamically into entry components.

The following is an example of specifying a bootstrapped component -

```
@NgModule({
  declarations: [
    AppComponent,
    LoginComponent
  ],
  imports: [
    BrowserModule,
    FormsModule,
    HttpModule,
    AppRoutingModule
```

```
  ],
  providers: [],
 bootstrap: [AppComponent]  // bootstrapped entry component
})
export class AppModule { }
```

The entry component is used to define components and created dynamically using the ComponentFactoryResolver.

The @NgModule.bootstrap property report the compiler that this is an entry component and it should generate code to bootstrap the application with this component.

2.5 When do I add components to entryComponents?

Most of the great application developers would not need to adds components to the entry components and Angular appends few components to entry components automatically.

Entry components are not tied to routes. They are loaded dynamically and are not referenced in component templates.

Chapter 3
Angular Directives

3.1 What Are Angular Directives?

Angular Directive is a TypeScript class which is declared as a @directive decorator. The directives allow you to attach behavior to DOM elements and the @directive decorator provide you an additional metadata that determines how directives should be processed, instantiated, and used at run-time.

3.2 What Are decorators?

The Decorators are the functions that modify JavaScript classes and it also used for attaching metadata to classes.

Directive decorator and metadata Properties -

```
@Directive({
    selector?: string
    inputs?: string[]
    outputs?: string[]
    host?: {...}
    providers?: Provider[]
    exportAs?: string
    queries?: {...}
})
```

Selector – It is a CSS selector that tells Angular to create an instance of this component wherever it finds the corresponding tag in template HTML.

```
For example, it is - <app-login></app-login>
```

CSS selector also triggers the instantiation of a directive.

The selector may be declared by element name, class name, attribute name, and attribute name & value.

Suppose we have a directive with an *<input type="checkbox">* selector and the HTML looks like this.

```
<form>
 <label>Name -</label> <input type="text">
 <label>Are you agree? </label> <input type="checkbox">
<form>
```

The directive will only be instantiated on the *<input type="checkbox">* element.

- **Inputs**– The list of class property names to data-bind as component inputs.
- **Outputs** - The list of class property names that expose output events that others can subscribe too.
- **Host**– These properties use to map the class property to host element bindings for properties, events, actions, and attributes.

The host looks like this.

```
@Directive({
  selector: 'button',
  host: {'(click)': 'onClick($event.target)'}
})
```

- **Providers** - list of providers available to this component and its children.
- **Queries**– To configure queries that can be injected into the component.

We have three types of Directives in Angular:

1. Component
2. Attribute Directives
3. Structural Directives

- **Components** - The component is a directive with their own templates and it is responsible for how a component should be processed, instantiated and used at runtime.
- **Structural Directives** - The structural directive is a directive and it is responsible for change the DOM layout by adding, removing, and manipulating elements.

  The most of the common built-in structural directives are NgIf, NgFor, and NgSwitch.
- **Attribute Directives** - The Attribute directive is a directive and it is responsible for change the behavior of a specified element or component.

3.3 What are the differences between @Component and @Directive?

The components are used, when you want to create new elements in the DOM with their own HTML template.

The attribute directives are used, when you want to change or update the existing elements in the DOM.

3.4 How to Create Custom Directives?

Let's start to create a simple directive.

We assume that you have installed the Angular CLI and all the necessary configurations are running in your app. Now, go to your project directory and execute the below CLI command for creating your custom directive –

```
ng g directive myCustom
```

After execute the above CLI command, created two files in the project - src/app folder

1. src/app/my-custom.directive.spec.ts
2. src/app/my-custom.directive.ts

And update files reference automatically in your project module – "src/app/app.module.ts"

Lest see in the code-sample, how it look like-

my-custom.directive.ts –

```
import { Directive } from '@angular/core';

@Directive({
  selector: '[appMyCustom]'
})
export class MyCustomDirective {
  constructor() { }
}
```

And app.module.ts –

```
import { MyCustomDirective } from './my-custom.directive'

//AppModule class with @NgModule decorator
@NgModule({
  //Static, this is the compiler configuration
  //declarations is used for configure the selectors.
  declarations: [
    AppComponent,
    MyCustomDirective,
  ],
  //Composability and Grouping
  //imports used for composing NgModules together.
  imports: [
    BrowserModule
  ],
  //Runtime or injector configuration
  //providers is used for runtime injector configuration.
  providers: [],
  //bootstrapped entry component
  bootstrap: [AppComponent]
})
export class AppModule { }
```

Chapter 4
Angular Modules

4.1 What Is Modules (NgModules)?

The NgModule is a TypeScript class marked by the @NgModule decorator.

The NgModule is a class and work with the @NgModule decorator function and also takes a metadata object that tells Angular how to compile and run module code.

The Angular module helps you to organize an application into associative blocks of functionality.

An angular module represents a core concept and plays a fundamental role in structuring Angular applications.

The NgModule is used to simplify the ways you define and manage the dependencies in your applications and also you can consolidate different components and services into associative blocks of functionality.

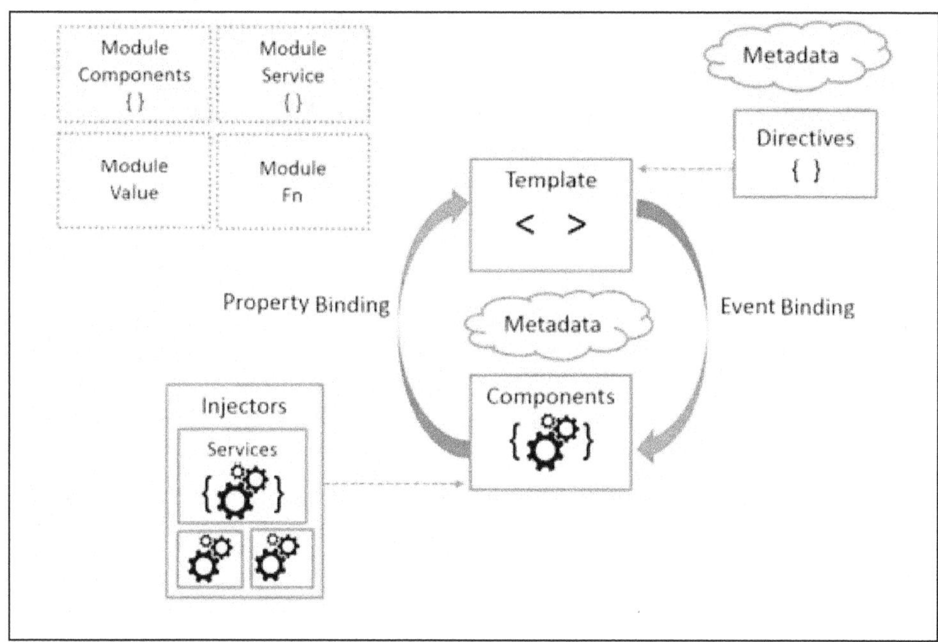

Every Angular application shou contains the components, service providers, pipes and other code files whose scope is defined by the containing NgModule.

The purpose of the module is to declare everything you create in Angular and group them together.

Every application has at least one Angular module, the root module that you bootstrap to launch the application. The Angular root module is called AppModule.

```
//JavaScript imports
import { BrowserModule } from '@angular/platform-browser';
import { NgModule } from '@angular/core';
                                              Importing Required Module
import { AppComponent } from './app.component';
import { LoginComponent } from './login/login.component';

//AppModule class with the @NgModule decorator.
@NgModule({
  declarations: [
    AppComponent,
    LoginComponent                      Defining NgModule Metadata Properties
  ],
  imports: [
    BrowserModule
  ],
  providers: [],
  bootstrap: [AppComponent]  // bootstrapped entry component
})
export class AppModule {
  //exporting moudle                        Exporting Moudle
}
```

The module is a way to organize your dependencies for:

1. Compiler
2. Dependency Injection

A module can import other modules and can expose its functionality to other modules. The modules can be loaded eagerly when the application starts or lazy loaded asynchronously by the router.

The angular loads a root dynamically because it is bootstrapped in the Angular Module.

An Angular app needs at least one module that serves as the root module.

You can use CLI commands to generate an app, the default AppModule is as follows:

```
ng new yourApp
```

The above CLI command is used to create a new Angular project and this CLI command automatically creates several folders and files which are necessary for project development, testing, configuration and so on.

The Angular CLI (Command Line Interface) is a tool to initialize, develop, scaffold and maintain Angular applications. To use this we need to install it first and it should be installed globally on your machine.

```
npm install -g @angular/cli
```

The following is an example of specifying a NgModule -

```
//JavaScript imports
import { BrowserModule } from '@angular/platform-browser';
import { NgModule } from '@angular/core';

import { AppComponent } from './app.component';
import { LoginComponent } from './login/login.component';

//AppModule class with @NgModule decorator.
@NgModule({
  declarations: [
    AppComponent,
    LoginComponent
  ],
  imports: [
    BrowserModule
  ],
  providers: [],
 bootstrap: [AppComponent]  // bootstrapped entry component
})
export class AppModule { }
```

4.2 What are the @NgModule Metadata Properties?

The @NgModule decorator identifies AppModule as a NgModule class.

The @NgModule takes a metadata object that tells Angular how to compile and launch the application.

The NgModule's important metadata properties are as follows:

1. providers
2. declarations
3. imports
4. exports
5. entryComponents
6. bootstrap
7. schemas
8. id

The @NgModule class with the decorator and metadata properties -

```
@NgModule({
  providers?: Provider[]
  declarations?: Array<Type<any> | any[]>
  imports?: Array<Type<any> | ModuleWithProviders | any[]>
  exports?: Array<Type<any> | any[]>
  entryComponents?: Array<Type<any> | any[]>
  bootstrap?: Array<Type<any> | any[]>
  schemas?: Array<SchemaMetadata | any[]>
  id?: string
})
```

Let understand in detail about NgModule metadata is as follows-

- **Providers:** A list of dependency injection (DI) providers and it defines the set of injectable objects that are available in the injector of this module.
- **Declarations**: A list of declarable classes, components, directives, and pipes that belong to this module. The compiler throws an error if you try to declare the same class in multiple modules.
- **Imports:** A list of modules and it used to import the supporting modules like FormsModule, RouterModule, CommonModule, or any other custom made feature module.
- **Exports:** A list of declarable components, directives, pipes, and modules which an importing module can use within a template of any component.
- **EntryComponents:** A list of components that should be compiled when this module is defined. By default, an Angular app always has at least one entry component, the root component, AppComponent.

  A bootstrapped component is an entry component that Angular loads into DOM during the application launch and other root components loaded dynamically into entry components.
- **Bootstrap:** A list of components that are automatically bootstrapped and the listed components will be added automatically to entryComponents.
- **Schemas:** Defines a schema that will allow any non-Angular elements and properties.
- **Id:** The Id is used to identify the modules in getModuleFactory. If left undefined, the NgModule will not be registered with getModuleFactory.

4.3 Why use multiple NgModules?

Multiple NgModules provides some potential benefits.

Actually, the modules help you to organize an application into associative blocks of functionality.

First one is organizing an application code. If you are putting around 99 resource files in the default app module and see the happing.

And the second one is - It opens the possibility of lazy loading via the router.

4.4 What Are the Purpose of @NgModule?

The NgModule is used to simplify the ways you define and manage the dependencies in your applications and also you can consolidate different components and services into cohesive blocks of functionality.

The @NgModule metadata divided into three categories as follows:

1. Static
2. Runtime
3. Composability/Grouping

- **Static:** It is a compiler configuration and configured via the declarations array.
- **Runtime:** It is injector configuration and configured via the provider's array.
- **Composability/Grouping:** Introducing NgModules together and configured via the imports and exports arrays.

The following is an example of specifying a NgModule metadata -

```
@NgModule({
  // Static, This is the compiler configuration
  declarations: [], //declarations is used for configure the
selectors.
  entryComponents: [], //entryComponents is used to generate
the host factory.

  //Runtime or injector configuration
  providers: [], // providers is used for runtime injector
configuration.

  //Composability and Grouping
  imports: [], // imports used for composing NgModules together.
  exports: [] //A list of declarations components, directives,
and pipes classes that an importing module can use.
})
```

4.5 What Types of NgModules?

There are four types of NgModules:

1. Features Module
2. Routing Module
3. Service Module
4. Widget Module
5. Shared Module

- **Features Module**: The feature modules are NgModules for the purpose of organizing an application code.
- **Routing Module:** The Routing is used to manage routes and also enables navigation from one view to another view as users perform application tasks.
- **Service Module:** The modules that only contain services and providers. It provides utility services such as data access and messaging. The root AppModule is the only module that should import service modules. The HttpClientModule is a good example of a service.
- **Widget Module:** The third party UI component libraries are widget modules.
- **Shared Module:** The shared module allows you to organize your application code. You can put your commonly used components, directives, and pipes into the one module and use whenever required to this module.

4.6 What Are the Types of Feature Modules?

There are five types of feature modules:

1. Domain Feature Modules
2. Routed Feature Modules
3. Routing Modules
4. Service Feature Modules
5. Widget Feature Modules

- **Routed Feature Module:** Routed feature modules are domain feature modules that components the targets of router navigation routes.

  A lazy-loaded routed feature module should not be imported by any module.

  Routed feature modules do not export anything because their components never appear in the template of an external component.
- **Routing Module:** A routing module provides routing configuration for another module and focus on:
  1. Defines Routes
  2. Adds Router Configuration to the module's imports
  3. Adds service providers to the module's providers
  4. A routing module doesn't have its own declarations. The components, directives, and pipes are the responsibility of the feature module and not the routing module.

  A routing module should only be imported by its companion module.
- **Service Feature Module:** Service modules provide utility services and used to communicate with the server. The HttpClientModule is a great example of a service module.

The root AppModule is the single module that should import service modules.

- **Domain Feature Module;** Domain feature modules deliver a user experience dedicated to a special application domain as like editing a customer and so on.
- **Widget Feature Module:** A widget module makes components, directives, and pipes available to external modules.

  The third party UI components and libraries are widget modules.

  Import widget modules in any module whose component templates need the widgets.

4.7 Why you use BrowserModule, CommonModule, FormsModule, RouterModule, and HttpClientModule?

- **BrowserModule:** The browser module is imported from @angular/platform-browser and it is used when you want to run your application in a browser.
- **CommonModule:** The common module is imported from @angular/common and it is used when you want to use directives - NgIf, NgFor and so on.
- **FormsModule:** The forms module is imported from @angular/forms and it is used when you build template driven forms.
- **RouterModule:** The router module is imported from @angular/router and is used for routing RouterLink, forRoot, and forChild.
- **HttpClientModule:** The HttpClientModule is imported from @angular/common/http and it is used to initiate HTTP request and responses in angular apps. The HttpClient is more modern and easy to use the alternative of HTTP.

4.8 What is the difference in NgModules and JavaScript Modules?

NgModules vs. JavaScript Modules

The NgModule is a TypeScript class decorated with @NgModule Decorator - is a fundamental feature of Angular.

JavaScript also has its own module system for managing collections of JavaScript objects. It is completely different from NgModule system.

In JavaScript, each file is a module and all objects are defined in the file belong to that module. The module declares some objects to be public by marking them with the export keyword.

Other JavaScript modules use import statements to access public objects from other modules.

The following is an example of specifying an export and import statements -

```
export class AppComponent { //...}
```

After export your class, you can import that file code in another file.

```
import { AppComponent } from './app.component';
```

Both the JavaScript and Angular use modules to organize applications code.

4.9 What classes should you not add to Module Declarations?

We do not declare - Modules, Services, objects, and non-angular helper classes in the module's declarations.

The Syntax for NgModule declaration array -

```
  declarations: [
    AppComponent,
    LoginComponent,
    MyPipe,
    MyDirective
  ]
```

The non-Angular classes and objects as following as -

1. Strings
2. Numbers
3. Functions
4. Entity Models
5. Configurations
6. and other helper classes

Note - You can use directives, components, and pipes classes in a module declaration.

The example of what goes into declarations array list –

```
//JavaScript imports directives, components, and pipes classes
import { BrowserModule } from '@angular/platform-browser';
import { NgModule } from '@angular/core';
import { AppComponent } from './app.component';
import { LoginComponent } from './login/login.component';
import { MyPipe } from './my-pipe.pipe';
import { MyDirective } from './my-directive.directive';
import {MySericeService} from './my-serice.service';
import{MyModuleModule} from '../app/my-module/my-
```

```
module.module';
//AppModule class with the @NgModule decorator.
@NgModule({
  declarations: [
    AppComponent,
    LoginComponent,
    MyPipe,
    MyDirective
  ],
  imports: [//DOM rendering, sanitization, and location
    BrowserModule
  ],
  providers: [//service providers
    MySericeService,
    MyModuleModule
  ],
  bootstrap: [AppComponent]  // bootstrapped entry component
})
export class AppModule {
  //exporting app module
}
```

In the above example, I have created and declared components, directives and pipes in the @NgModule class using the CLI commands.

1. ng g component my-component
2. ng g pipe my-pipe
3. ng g directive my-directive
4. ng g service mySerice
5. ng g module myModule

These CLI commands automatically imported components, directives, and pipes classes inside the module.

4.10 Should you import BrowserModule or CommonModule?

BrowserModule – Most of all browser applications should import BrowserModule from *@angular/platform-browser* and the BrowserModule provides services that are important to launch and run your browser apps.

Do not import BrowserModule in any other module.

BrowserModule also re-exports *CommonModule* from *@angular/common* and CommonModule is used when you want to use directives - NgIf, NgFor and may more.

BrowserModule exports a couple of NgModules like -

```
exports: [
  CommonModule,
  ApplicationModule
]
```

And

```
//AppModule class with the @NgModule decorator
@NgModule({
  declarations: [
    AppComponent,
    LoginComponent,
    MyPipe,
    MyDirective
  ],
  imports: [//DOM rendering, sanitization, and location
    BrowserModule
  ],
  providers: [//service providers
    MySericeService,
    MyModuleModule
  ],
 bootstrap: [AppComponent],  // bootstrapped entry component
  exports: [
    CommonModule,
    ApplicationModule
  ]
})
export class AppModule {
  //exporting app module
}
```

4.11 What happens if you Import the same module twice?

You can import the same module twice but Angular does not like modules with circular references and raise the circular dependency warnings on builds.

Actually, the module helps you to organize an application into associative blocks of functionality.

For example – Class-A and Class-B can be in the same file if needed. This warning is not an opinion on bad behavior.

4.12 What kinds of modules should I have and how should I use them?

Every app is different. Developers have various levels of experience and comfort with the available choices.

Some suggestions and guidelines appear to have broad appeal.

1. SharedModule
2. CoreModule
3. Feature Modules - Domain, Routed, Routing, Service, and Widget

4.13 Why is it bad if a shared module provides a service to a lazy-loaded module?

The lazily loaded scenario causes your app to create a new instance every time, instead of using the singleton.

Lazy loading is the best practice of loading expensive resources on-demand. This can greatly reduce the initial startup time for single page web applications (SPA). Instead of downloading all the application code and resources before the app starts, they are fetched just-in-time (JIT), as needed.

The eagerly loaded scenario your app to create a singleton, instead of creates a new instance every time.

Chapter 5

Angular Form, Templates, and Validations

5.1 What are the Validator functions?

There are two types of validator functions which are:

1. Async validators
2. Sync validators

Async validator functions take a control instance and return an observable that later emits a set of validation errors or null.

Sync validator functions take a control instance and return a set of validation errors or null.

Angular runs only Async validators due to some performance issues.

5.2 What Is a Template Reference variable?

A template reference variable is a way of capturing a reference to a specific element, component, directive, and pipe so that it can be used in the same template HTML.

You should declare a reference variable by using the hash symbol (#).

The Angular components and directives only match selectors for classes that are declared in the Angular module.

Template Reference Variable Syntax –

You can use a template reference variable by two ways.

1. Using hash symbol (#)
2. Using reference symbol (ref-)

The following examples of specifying a template reference variable using Input Text Box –

I have declared a reference variable "cellnumber" using the **hash symbol (#)** and **reference symbol (ref-)**.

```
<input type="text" ref-cellnumber> //cellnumber will be a
template reference variable.
```

And

```
<input #cellnumber placeholder="Cell number"> //cellnumber
will be a template reference variable.
```

A reference to the input element is created that can be used later on in my template and the scope for "**cellnumber**" variable is the entire HTML template in which the reference is defined.

To use reference to get the value of the input for instance –

```
//cellnumber refers to the input element
<button (click)="show(cellnumber)">click to see</button>
```

In the below line of code, the variable "cellnumber" refer to the HTMLElement object instance for the input -

```
show(cellnumber: HTMLInputElement){
  console.log(cellnumber.value);
}
```

You can use the ViewChild decorator to reference it inside your component.

```
import {ViewChild, ElementRef} from '@angular/core';

// Reference cellnumber variable inside Component
@ViewChild('cellnumber') cellInputRef: ElementRef;
```

And finally, you can use this.nameInputRef anywhere inside your component class.

```
show(){
  this.contactNumber = this.cellInputRef.nativeElement.value
}
```

5.3 Template Reference Variable with NgForm

Here we will discuss about how to access NgForm directive using template reference variable.

```
<form     (ngSubmit)="onSubmitEmployee(empForm)"
#empForm="ngForm">
   <label>F-Name </label><input name="f-name" required
[(ngModel)]="employee.fname">
   <label>L-Name </label><input name="l-name" required
[(ngModel)]="employee.lname">
   <label>Age      </label><input name="age" required
```

```
[(ngModel)]="employee.age">

                    <button          type="submit"
[disabled]="!empForm.form.valid">Submit</button>
</form>
```

In the above NgForm example contains a ngSubmit event and form directive.

The ngSubmit – The ngSubmit directive specifies a function to run when the form is submitted. Here on form submit onSubmitEmployee component method will be called.

The NgForm - It is a nestable alias of form directive. The main purpose of ngForm is to group the controls, but not a replacement of <form> tag.

HTML does not allow nesting of form elements. It is very useful to nest forms.

5.4 How to bind to user input events to Component event Handlers?

Most of the DOM events are triggered by user input and bind to these events provides a way to get inputs from a user.

The following example shows a click event binding – [on-click.component.ts]

```
import { Component, OnInit } from '@angular/core';

@Component({
  selector: 'app-on-click',
  templateUrl: './on-click.component.html',
  styleUrls: ['./on-click.component.css']
})
export class OnClickComponent implements OnInit {

  welcomeMsg = '';
  constructor() { }

  ngOnInit() { }

  onClick() {
    this.welcomeMsg = 'Welcome you, Anil!';
  }
}
```

And on-click.component.html -

```
<div class="msg">
  <button (click)="onClick()">Click Me!</button>
  <p>
    {{welcomeMsg}}
  </p>
</div>
```

OR

```
<!— Canonical form, the (on-) prefix alternative —>
<div class="msg">
  <button on-click="onClick($event)">Click Me!</button>
  <p>
    {{welcomeMsg}}
  </p>
</div>
```

When the user clicks the button, Angular calls the onClick method from OnClickComponent.

5.5 How to get user input from the $event object?

The DOM events carry all information that is useful to the component.

The following example shows to get user input from the $event – key-up.component.ts

```
import { Component, OnInit } from '@angular/core';

@Component({
  selector: 'app-key-up',
  templateUrl: './key-up.component.html',
  styleUrls: ['./key-up.component.css']
})
export class KeyUpComponent implements OnInit {

  values = '';
  constructor() { }

  ngOnInit() { }

  //KeyUp events.
  onKeyUp(event: any) {
    this.values += event.target.value + ' : ';
  }
}
```

And key-up.component.html –

```
<div class="event">
  <button (click)="onKeyUp($event)">KeyUp Event!</button>
  <p>
    {{values}}
  </p>
</div>
```

5.6 How to get user input from a Template Reference Variable?

This is the other way to get the user data. It is also called #var.

"A template reference variable is mostly a reference to a DOM element within a template. It can also be a reference to Angular components or directives and others."

It looks like this.

```
<input #name placeholder="Enter Name">
```

The following example shows to get user input from a template reference variable - template- reference.component.ts

```
import { Component, OnInit } from '@angular/core';

@Component({
  selector: 'app-template-reference',
  templateUrl: './template-reference.component.html',
  styleUrls: ['./template-reference.component.css']
})
export class TemplateReferenceComponent implements OnInit {

  constructor() { }

  ngOnInit() {
  }
}
```

And template-reference.component.html –

```
<div class="event">
  <button #keydownVal (keydown)="0"></button>
  <p>
    {{keydownVal.value}}
  </p>
</div>
```

5.7 How to Create a Custom Validator for both Model Driven and template driven forms?

There are two types of Validators –

1. Built-in Validators
2. Custom Model Form Validators
    a. Email Validator
    b. Password Validator
    c. Secure Site Validator
    d. Credit card validator

Built-in Validators -

1. **Validators .required:** Requires a form control to have a non-empty value.
2. **Validators .minlength:** Requires a form control to have a value of a min length.
3. **Validators .maxlength:** Requires a form control to have a value of a max length.
4. **Validators .pattern:** Requires a form control's value to match a given regex.

Built-in validator looks like –

```
this.empForm = new FormGroup({
                              'email':               new
FormControl(this.employee.email,[Validators.required,
ValidationService.emailValidator]),
    'name': new FormControl(this.employee.name,
[Validators.required,Validators.minLength(4)]), 'Dep': new
FormControl(this.employee.Dep, [Validators.required,
Validators.minLength(10)]),          'Desc':       new
FormControl(this.employee.Desc, [Validators.required,
Validators.minLength(100),Validators.minLength(500)]),
});
```

5. **Custom Model Form Validators:** Validators are core functions, they take as input a FormControl instance and returns either null if it's valid or flag for errors.

You can use the custom validator to validate a specific requirement like:

1. Email Validator
2. Password Validator
3. Secure Site Validator
4. Credit card validator
5. And may more

The Following Steps involve CREATING custom validators –

Steps 1- Create validation service using the CLI command.

```
ng g service validation
```

Steps 2 - import validation service in your app NgModule –

```
import { BrowserModule } from '@angular/platform-browser';
import { NgModule } from '@angular/core';
import {FormsModule, FormGroup} from '@angular/forms';
import {RouterModule} from '@angular/router';
import {HttpClientModule} from "@angular/common/http";
//MY COMPONENTS
import { AppComponent } from './app.component';
import { LoginComponent } from './login/login.component';
import { RegisterComponent } from './register/
register.component';
import { EmployeeComponent } from './employee/
employee.component';

//My Services
import { AuthServiceService } from './auth-service.service';
import { AuthGuard } from './auth.guard';
import { EmployeeService} from './employee.service';
import { ValidationService } from './validation.service';

@NgModule({
  declarations: [
    AppComponent,
    LoginComponent,
    RegisterComponent,
    EmployeeComponent
  ],
  imports: [
    BrowserModule,
    FormsModule,
    HttpClientModule,
    RouterModule.forRoot([
      { path: '', component: AppComponent, pathMatch: 'full'
},
       { path: 'register', component: RegisterComponent },
       { path: 'employee', component: EmployeeComponent},
       { path: 'login', component: LoginComponent}])
  ],
  providers: [EmployeeService, ValidationService],
  bootstrap: [AppComponent]
})
export class AppModule { }
```

Steps 3 - Write the customer validation method in your validation.service.ts - import { Injectable } from '@angular/core';

```
@Injectable()
export class ValidationService {

  constructor() { }

  //Check Site contains SSL Security protocol  or Not.
  static secureSiteValidator(control){
       if (!control.value.startsWith('https') ||
!control.value.includes('.in')) {
      return { IsSecureSite: true };
    }

    return null;
  }

  //Email Validator
  static emailValidator(control) {
       if (control.value.match(/[a-z0-9!#$%&'*+/=?^_`{|}~-
]+(?:\.[a-z0-9!#$%&'*+/=?^_`{|}~-]+)*@(?:[a-z0-9](?:[a-z0-9-
]*[a-z0-9])?\.)+[a-z0-9](?:[a-z0-9-]*[a-z0-9])?/)) {
          return null;
      }
      else {
          return { 'InvalidEmail': true };
      }
  }

  //Password Validator
  static passwordValidator(control) {
         if (control.value.match(/^(?=.*[0-9])[a-zA-Z0-
9!@#$%^&*]{6,100}$/)) {
          return null;
      }
      else {
          return { 'InvalidPassword': true };
      }
  }
}
```

Steps 4 - Use of validation service in your components and its looks like –

```
import { Component, OnInit } from '@angular/core';
import {Employee } from '../employee'
import { Validators, FormGroup, FormControl } from '@angular/
forms';
import {EmployeeService} from '../employee.service'
import { ValidationService } from '../validation.service';

@Component({
  selector: 'app-employee',
  templateUrl: './employee.component.html',
  styleUrls: ['./employee.component.css']
})
export class EmployeeComponent implements OnInit {

  constructor( public _empService: EmployeeService) { }
  empForm:any;

  ngOnInit() {
    this.empForm = new FormGroup({
                                          'email':      new
FormControl(this.employee.email,[Validators.required,
ValidationService.emailValidator]),
          'name': new FormControl(this.employee.name,
[Validators.required,Validators.minLength(4)]),
          'Dep': new FormControl(this.employee.Dep,
[Validators.required, Validators.minLength(10)]),
          'Desc': new FormControl(this.employee.Desc,
[Validators.required, Validators.minLength(100),
Validators.minLength(500)]),
    });
  }

  employee = new Employee(0,'','','','','');
  submitted = false;

  //Add new Employee
  onSubmit() {
    this.submitted = true;
                                  let       isSuccess       =
this._empService.addEmployee(this.employee);
    if(isSuccess){
     //handle success
     console.log(isSuccess);
```

```
    }else{
      //handle errors
    }
  }
}
```

And

```
<div class="container">
  <h1>Employee Form</h1>
  <form #empForm="ngForm" (ngSubmit)="onSubmit()">
      <div class="form-group">
          <label for="name">Email</label>
         <input type="text" class="form-control" id="email"
required [(ngModel)]="employee.email" name="email">
        </div>
    <div class="form-group">
      <label for="name">Name</label>
        <input type="text" class="form-control" id="name"
required [(ngModel)]="employee.name" name="name">
    </div>

    <div class="form-group">
      <label for="Dep">Department</label>
         <input type="text" class="form-control" id="Dep"
required [(ngModel)]="employee.Dep" name="Dep">
    </div>

    <div class="form-group">
      <label for="Desc">Desc</label>
        <input type="text" class="form-control" id="Desc"
required [(ngModel)]="employee.Desc" name="Desc">
    </div>

       <button type="submit" class="btn btn-success"
[disabled]="!empForm.form.valid">Submit</button>
  </form>

  <div [hidden]="!submitted">
     <h4 style="color:green;">Record Added Successfully!</
h4>
  </div>
</div>
```

Chapter 6
Angular Elements

6.1 What're Angular Elements?

Angular Element is a package which is part of the Angular framework- @angular/elements and it was introduced in Angular 6 and hopefully, this will improve with Angular 7 or higher versions.

Angular Elements was the brainchild of Angular's and it is one of the most anticipated features of Angular 6 release.

Angular 6 will be the first release that fully supports Angular elements.

Angular elements will give you the ability to use your Angular components in other environments like jQuery app or Vue.js app or anything else.

It is very useful, especially when you are working with dynamically loaded HTML code.

It also offers functionality that allows you to convert a normal Angular component to a native web component.

Angular Elements give you an easy way to implement a web standard.

Custom Elements, lets you to create custom tags in a framework-agnostic way. They let you to reuse your Angular components in any webpage. Yes, you can embed Angular Elements inside a React.js or Vue.js page without any knowledge of Angular.

Custom Elements remove the need to rewrite a widget every-time a new framework pops up.

6.2 How do Angular Elements work?

1. They are self-Bootstrapping.
2. They host the Angular Component inside a Custom Element.
3. They act as a bridge between the DOM APIs and Angular Components.
4. Anyone can use your component without having to know Angular.

6.3 What are the *features of Angular Elements?*

The features of Angular Elements:

1. Self-bootstrapping.
2. Hosts an Angular Component inside Custom Elements.
3. A bridge between DOM and Angular Components APIs.

6.4 What are Advantages of Angular Elements?

Advantages of Angular Elements -

1. Reusability - Reuse components across your apps.
2. Widgets – You can use Angular components in other environments.
3. CMS Pages.

6.5 How to Install Angular Elements?

To add support for Angular Elements use the Angular CLI command - **ng add**.

```
ng add @angular/elements
```

6.6 What Is "ng add" for Angular Elements?

The "ng add" command is built on schematics. When you run ng add @angular/elements the CLI scans your project and updates your code to support Angular Elements.

It is automatic. There's no manual configuration required.

Once it is successfully added in your project, then

Two dependencies are added to the package.json which are:

1. @angular/elements: "^6.0.1
2. document-register-element: ^1.7.2

6.7 Can you show me an example of an Angular Element?

Simply you can create a normal Angular component with inputs & outputs and import this component inside your angular module with the help of @angular/elements.

Now, your elements are ready to use inside a simple HTML page.

```
<my-custom-elmet message="This is my custom element "></my-custom-elmet>
```

Chapter 7
Dependency Injection (DI)

7.1 What Is a Dependency?

When module X in an application needs module Y to run, then module Y has a dependency of module X.

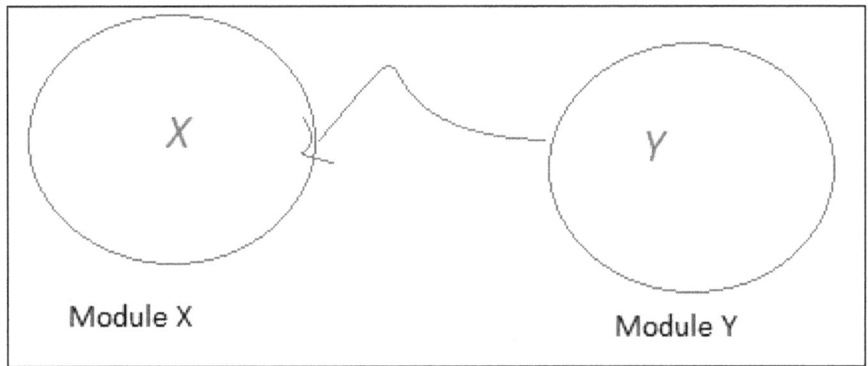

7.2 What Is Dependency Injection (DI)?

Dependency Injection is a powerful pattern for managing code dependencies. DI is a way to create objects that depend upon other objects.

Angular has its own DI framework pattern, and you can't build an Angular application without Dependency injection (DI).

A DI system supplies the dependent objects when it creates an instance of an object.

Let us take an example of a CAR. The CAR consists of:

1. Wheel
2. Headlight
3. Outer door
4. Inner door
5. Glass
6. Window
7. Fuel level sensor

So to complete the CAR, we need these things.

In this example, we need to require total seven and many more classes to build a fully functional CAR.

1. Car class
2. Wheel class
3. Headlight class
4. Outer door class
5. Inner door class
6. Glass class
7. Window class
8. Fuel level sensor class

Let's see what happen, without Dependency Injection (DI)

To complete the CAR class, we need to import all these eight classes here and make one fully functional CAR.

Now, here we have created eight classes instance in the constructor of CAR class.

Note that, the CAR class is totally dependent on these eight classes. Otherwise, it will not complete the CAR.

We are creating the instances in the CAR constructor. So Wheel, Headlight, Outer door, Inner door, Glass, Window, and Fuel are not decoupled from the CAR class.

Let's see what happen, with Dependency Injection (DI)

If we are using Dependency Injection then, we do not need to create the instances in the constructor.

First, we need to provide all the dependencies to the "*app.module.ts*" class -

```
import { BrowserModule } from '@angular/platform-browser';
import { NgModule } from '@angular/core';

//Import App Component
import { AppComponent } from './app.component';

//Import CAR classes.
import {Wheel} from './car/wheel';
import {Headlight} from './car/headlight';
import {Glass} from './car/glass';
import {InnerDoor} from './car/inner-door';
import {OuterDoor} from './car/outer-door';
import {Window} from './car/window';
import {FuelLevel} from './car/fuel-level';

//AppModule class with @NgModule decorator.
@NgModule({
  //Static, This is the compiler configuration
```

```
  //declarations is used for configure the selectors.
  declarations: [
    AppComponent,
  ],

  //Composability and Grouping
  // imports used for composing NgModules together.
  imports: [
    BrowserModule
  ],

  //Runtime or injector configuration
  //providers is used for runtime injector configuration.
 providers: [Wheel, Headlight, Glass, InnerDoor, OuterDoor,
Window, FuelLevel],

  //bootstrapped entry component
  bootstrap: [AppComponent]
})
export class AppModule { }
```

In providers array, we need to provide all eight dependencies.

Then, In the CAR class, inject those dependencies into CAR constructor:

```
import {Wheel} from './car/wheel';
import {Headlight} from './car/headlight';
import {Glass} from './car/glass';
import {InnerDoor} from './car/inner-door';
import {OuterDoor} from './car/outer-door';
import {Window} from './car/window';
import {FuelLevel} from './car/fuel-level';

export class Car {
    constructor(public wheel: Wheel,
                public headlight: Headlight,
                public glass: Glass,
                public innerdoor: InnerDoor,
                public outerdoor: OuterDoor,
                public window: Window,
                public fuellevel: FuelLevel) {}

}
```

When CAR instance is created, at that time all the other instances of other classes are also created.

7.3 What Is Dependency Injection Pattern?

DI is an application design pattern and you really cannot build an Angular application without dependency injection (DI).

7.4 What Is Injectors?

A service is just a class in Angular until you register with an Angular dependency injector.

The injector is responsible for creating angular service instances and injecting them into classes.

You rarely create an injector yourself and Angular creates automatically during the bootstrap process.

Angular doesn't know automatically how you want to create instances of your services or injector. You must configure it by specifying providers for every service. Actually, providers tell the injector how to create the service and without a provider we are not able to create the service.

Bootstrap defines the components that should be bootstrapped when this module is bootstrapped. The components listed here will automatically be added to entryComponents.

7.5 What Are @Injectable providers?

The @Injectable decorator identifies services and other classes that are intended to be injected. It can also be used to configure a provider for those services.

To inject the service into a component, Angular provides an Injector decorator: @Injectable().

A provider defines the set of injectable objects that are available in the injector of this module.

The @Injectable decorator marks a class as available to an injector for instantiation. An injector reports an error when trying to instantiate a class that is not marked as @Injectable.

Injectors are also responsible for instantiating components. At the run-time, the injectors can read class metadata in the JavaScript code and use the constructor parameter type information to determine what things to inject.

Injectable decorator and metadata:

```
@Injectable({
  providedIn?: Type<any> | 'root' | null
  factory: () => any
})
```

To inject the service into a component, Angular provides an Injector decorator: @Injectable().

Here we configure a provider for CustomerService by using the @Injectable decorator on the class.

We have the following steps to create a Service:

1. Create the service class.
2. Define the metadata with a decorator.
3. Import what we need.

In the above example, providedIn tells Angular that the root injector is responsible for creating an instance of the CustomerService.

The Angular CLI sets up provider automatically when you generating a new service.

7.6 Why @Inject()?

The @Inject is a special technique for letting Angular knows that a parameter must be injected.

Inject decorator and metadata:

```
@Inject({
  token: any
})
```

When @Inject () is not present, Injector will use the type annotation of the parameter.

```
import { Component, OnInit, Inject } from '@angular/core';
import { HttpClient } from '@angular/common/http';

@Component({
  selector: 'app-customer',
  templateUrl: './customer.component.html',
  styleUrls: ['./customer.component.css']
})

export class CustomerComponent implements OnInit {

  constructor(@Inject(HttpClient) private http) {
    // use this.http which is the Http provider.
  }

  ngOnInit(){ }
}
```

At this point, @Inject is a manual way of specifying this lookup token, followed by the lowercase HTTP argument to tell Angular what to assign it against.

7.7 What Is Hierarchical Dependency Injectors?

Angular has a Hierarchical Dependency Injection system. There is actually a tree of injectors that are parallel of application's component tree. You can reconfigure the injectors at any level of that component tree.

7.8 What Is Injector Tree?

In the Dependency Injection guide, you learned how to configure a dependency injector and how to retrieve dependencies where you need them.

An application may have multiple injectors. An Angular application is a tree of components. Each component instance has its own injector. The tree of components parallels the tree of injectors.

Three level component tree:

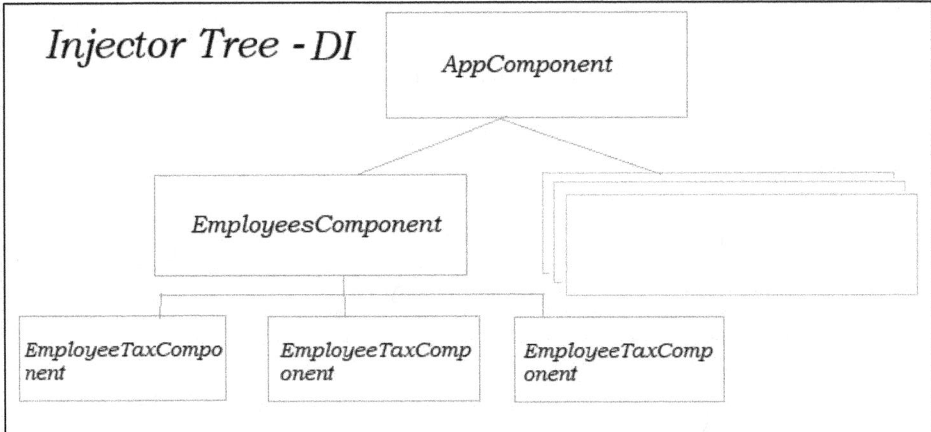

Chapter 8
HttpClient

8.1 What is HttpClient in Angular? What is the role and responsibility of HttpClient?

HttpClient is performing HTTP requests and responses.

Most of all web applications communicate with backend services over the HTTP protocol and all modern browsers support two different APIs for making HTTP requests i.e.

1. XMLHttpRequest interface
2. fetch() APIs

The HttpClient is easy to use, as an alternative of HTTP.

HttpClient is an improved replacement for HTTP. They expect to deprecate http in Angular 5 and remove it in a later version.

The new HttpClient service is included in the HTTP Client Module that is used to initiate HTTP request and responses in angular apps. The HttpClientModule is a replacement of HttpModule.

HttpClient also gives us advanced functionality like the ability to listen for progress events and interceptors to modify requests or responses.

Before using the HttpClient, you must need to import the Angular HttpClientModule and the HttpClientModule is imported from *@angular/common/http*.

You must import HttpClientModule after BrowserModule in your angular apps.

First, you'll need to imported HttpClientModule from @angular/common/http in your app module and it must be import HttpClientModule after BrowserModule in your angular apps.

Consider the following example:

```
import { BrowserModule } from '@angular/platform-browser';
import { NgModule } from '@angular/core';
import { HttpClientModule } from '@angular/common/http';

//Import App Component
import { AppComponent } from './app.component';
```

```
//AppModule class with @NgModule decorator
@NgModule({
  imports: [
    BrowserModule,
    //import HttpClientModule after BrowserModule
    HttpClientModule,
  ],
  //Static, compiler configuration
  //declarations is used for configure the selectors
  declarations: [
    AppComponent,
  ],
  //Runtime or injector configuration
  providers: [],
  //bootstrapped entry component
  bootstrap: [ AppComponent ]
})
export class AppModule {}
```

After importing HttpClientModule into the AppModule, you can inject the HttpClient into your created service.

Consider the following example:

```
import { Injectable } from '@angular/core';
import { HttpClient } from '@angular/common/http';

@Injectable()
export class CustomerService {

  //Inject HttpClient into your components or services
  constructor(private httpClient: HttpClient) { }

}
```

HttpClient supports mutating a request, which is, sending data to the server with HTTP methods such as PUT, POST, and DELETE.

HttpClient is use the XMLHttpRequest browser API to execute HTTP request.

HttpClient Perform HTTP requests:

1. GET method – get()
2. POST method – post()
3. PUT method – put()
4. DELETE method – delete()
5. HEAD method – head()

6. JSONP method – jsonp()
7. OPTIONS method – options()
8. PATCH method – patch()

And the HttpClient class looks like:

```
class HttpClient {
  constructor(handler: HttpHandler)
   request(first: string | HttpRequest<any>, url?: string,
options: {...}): Observable<any>
  delete(url: string, options: {...}): Observable<any>
  get(url: string, options: {...}): Observable<any>
  head(url: string, options: {...}): Observable<any>
  jsonp<T>(url: string, callbackParam: string): Observable<T>
  options(url: string, options: {...}): Observable<any>
   patch(url: string, body: any | null, options: {...}):
Observable<any>
   post(url: string, body: any | null, options: {...}):
Observable<any>
   put(url: string, body: any | null, options: {...}):
Observable<any>
}
```

The options contain the list of parameters:

1. headers,
2. observe,
3. params,
4. reportProgress,
5. responseType,
6. withCredentials

The following options parameters look like:

```
  options: {
    headers?: HttpHeaders | {
         [header: string]: string | string[];
    };
    observe?: 'body';
    params?: HttpParams | {
         [param: string]: string | string[];
    };
    reportProgress?: boolean;
    responseType: 'blob';
    withCredentials?: boolean;
  }
```

Benefits of HttpClient:

1. HttpClient include the testability features.
2. HttpClient include typed request.
3. HttpClient include response objects.
4. HttpClient include request and response interception.
5. HttpClient include Observable APIs.
6. HttpClient include error handling.

8.2 What Is HttpInterceptor?

HttpInterceptors is an interface which uses to implement the intercept method.

Intercepts HttpRequest and handles them.

Intercepts is an advanced feature that allows us to intercept each request/ response and modify it before sending/receiving.

Interceptors capture every request and manipulate it before sending and also catch every response and process it before completing the call.

Firstly, we can implement own interceptor service and this service will "catch" each request and append an Authorization header.

You can see this in the following example:

```
import {Injectable} from '@angular/core';
import {HttpEvent, HttpInterceptor, HttpHandler, HttpRequest}
from '@angular/common/http';

@Injectable()
export class MyInterceptor implements HttpInterceptor {
  //Intercepts HttpRequest and handles them.
   intercept(req: HttpRequest<any>, next: HttpHandler):
Observable<HttpEvent<any>> {
         const reqHeader = req.clone({headers:
req.headers.set('Authorization', 'MyAuthToken')});

    return next.handle(reqHeader);
  }
}
```

After that you can configure your own interceptor service (MyInterceptor) and HTTP_INTERCEPTORS in the app Module.

```
import {NgModule} from '@angular/core';
import {HTTP_INTERCEPTORS} from '@angular/common/http';

@NgModule({
  providers: [{
```

```
    provide: HTTP_INTERCEPTORS,
    useClass: MyInterceptor,
    multi: true,
  }],
})
export class AppModule {}
```

By following this logic, Authorization token will be appended to each request. It is also possible to override request's headers by using **set**() method.

8.3 What's the difference between HttpModule and HttpClientModule?

HttpClientModule -

The HttpClientModule imported form -

```
import { HttpClientModule } from '@angular/common/http';
```

NgModule which provides the HttpClient and is associated with components services and the interceptors can be added to the chain behind HttpClient by binding them to the multi-provider for HTTP_INTERCEPTORS.

HttpModule –

Http deprecate @angular/http in favour of @angular/common/http.

HttpModule imported from –

```
import { HttpModule } from '@angular/http';
```

They both support HTTP calls but HTTP is the older API and will eventually be deprecated.

The new HttpClient service is included in the HttpClientModule that is used to initiate HTTP request and responses in angular apps. The HttpClientModule is a replacement of HttpModule.

8.4 What's the difference between HTTP and HttpClient?

The HttpClient is used to perform HTTP requests and it is imported form @angular/common/http.

The HttpClient is easy to use as an alternative of HTTP.

HttpClient is an improved replacement for Http. They expect to deprecate Http in Angular 5 and remove it in a later version.

It's an upgraded version of http from @angular/http module with the following improvements:

1. Immutable request and response objects.
2. Interceptors allow middleware logic to be inserted into the pipeline.

3. Progress events for both request and response.
4. Typed.
5. Event firing.
6. Synchronous response body access.
7. Support JSON body types and JSON by default and now, no need to be explicitly parsed.
8. Automatic conversion from JSON to an object.
9. Post request verification.
10. A flush based testing framework.
11. Simplified syntax for headers.

The example with HttpClient:

```
import { Injectable } from '@angular/core';
import { HttpClient } from '@angular/common/http';

@Injectable()
export class CustomerService {

  //Inject HttpClient into your components or services
  constructor(private http: HttpClient) { }
}
```

And other example with Http:

```
import { Injectable } from '@angular/core';
import { Http } from '@angular/http';

@Injectable()
export class CustomerService {

  //Inject HttpClient into your components or services
  constructor(private http: Http) { }
}
```

8.5 What Are HttpHeaders?

The Http Headers is immutable Map and each and every set() returns a new instance and applies the changes with lazy parsing.

An immutable set of Http headers, with lazy parsing.

HttpHeaders Constructor -

```
constructor(headers?: string | { [name: string]: string |
string[];});
```

Imports HttpHeaders from:

```
import {HttpHeaders } from '@angular/common/http';
```

HttpHeaders class contains the list of methods:

1. has() - Checks for existence of header by given name.
2. get() - Returns the first header that matches given name.
3. keys() - Returns the names of the headers.
4. getAll() - Returns list of header values for a given name.
5. append() - Append headers by chaining.
6. set() - To set a custom header on the request for a given name.
7. delete() - To delete the header on the request for a given name.

8.6 How to set a custom header on the request?

To set a custom header on the request, firstly we need to instantiate HttpHeaders() object and pass ('header', 'value') into a function.

```
let headers = new HttpHeaders().set('Content-Type', 'text');
```

In the above example we set "Content-Type" header value to be "text" and the default header "Content-Type" is – "application/json"

It is a type of immutable Map so if you assign a new value it will reinitialize the object.

```
let requestHeaders = new HttpHeaders().set('Content-Type',
'application/json');
requestHeaders = requestHeaders.set('authorization', 'Bearer
' + token);
```

We can also append headers by chaining HttpHeaders() constructor and will look like this-

```
let requestheaders = new HttpHeaders().set('Content-Type',
'application/json')
                    .set('authorization', 'Bearer ' + token);
```

And final request with custom headers will look like this –

```
import { Injectable } from '@angular/core';
import { HttpClient, HttpHeaders } from '@angular/common/
http';

@Injectable()
export class CustomerService {
```

```
  //Inject HttpClient into your components or services
  constructor(private http: HttpClient) { }

  //Set Headers
   requestHeaders  =  new  HttpHeaders().set('Content-Type',
'text')
                                  .append('Authorization',
'CustomToke_AFA96A3429A9524');

  //Get Customer list
  getCustomers() {
    this.http.get('https://code-sample.com/customerjson', {
         headers: this.requestHeaders
     }).map((data:HttpEvent<object>) => { console.log(data)
})
  }
}
```

8.7 How to catch and log specific Angular errors in your app?

The default implementation of ErrorHandler log error messages, status, and stack to the console. To intercept error handling, we write a custom exception handler that replaces this default as appropriate for your app.

```
import { Injectable, ErrorHandler } from '@angular/core';
import {ErrorLoggService} from './error-logg.service';

// Global error handler for logging errors
@Injectable()
export class GlobalErrorHandler extends ErrorHandler {
    constructor(private errorLogService: ErrorLoggService)
{
        //Angular provides a hook for centralized exception
handling.
        //constructor ErrorHandler(): ErrorHandler
         super();
    }

    handleError(error) : void {
        this.errorLogService.logError(error);
    }
}
```

8.8 How to create a custom ErrorHandler?

The best way to log exceptions is to provide a specific log message for each possible exception. Always ensure that sufficient information is being logged and that nothing important is being excluded.

The multiple steps involved in creating custom error logging in Angular:

1. Create a constant class for global error messages.
2. Create an error log service – ErrorLoggService.
3. Create a global error handler for using the error log service for logging errors.

Steps 1 – In the first step, we will create a constant class for logging global error messages and it will look like this.

```
export class AppConstants {
   public static get baseURL(): string { return 'http://
localhost:4200/api'; }
  public static get httpError(): string { return 'There was
an HTTP error.'; }
  public static get typeError(): string { return 'There was
a Type error.'; }
  public static get generalError(): string { return 'There
was a general error.'; }
   public static get somethingHappened(): string { return
'Nobody threw an Error but something happened!'; }
}
```

Steps 2 – In the second steps, we will create an error log service (ErrorLoggService) for error logging and it will look like this.

```
import { Injectable} from '@angular/core';
import { HttpErrorResponse } from '@angular/common/http';
import{ AppConstants} from '../app/constants'

//#region Handle Errors Service
@Injectable()
export class ErrorLoggService {

  constructor() {  }

  //Log error method
  logError(error: any) {
    //Returns a date converted to a string using Universal
Coordinated Time (UTC).
    const date = new Date().toUTCString();
```

```
    if (error instanceof HttpErrorResponse) {
      //The response body may contain clues as to what went
wrong
          console.error(date, AppConstants.httpError,
error.message, 'Status code:',
                (<HttpErrorResponse>error).status);
    }
    else if (error instanceof TypeError) {
          console.error(date, AppConstants.typeError,
error.message, error.stack);
    }
    else if (error instanceof Error) {
          console.error(date, AppConstants.generalError,
error.message, error.stack);
    }
    else if(error instanceof ErrorEvent){
      //A client-side or network error occurred. Handle it
accordingly
          console.error(date, AppConstants.generalError,
error.message);
    }
    else {
        console.error(date, AppConstants.somethingHappened,
error.message, error.stack);
    }
  }
}
//#endregion
```

Steps 3 – In the 3rd steps, we will create a global error handler for using the error log service for logging errors and it will look like this.

```
import { Injectable, ErrorHandler } from '@angular/core';
import {ErrorLoggService} from './error-logg.service';

// Global error handler for logging errors
@Injectable()
export class GlobalErrorHandler extends ErrorHandler {
    constructor(private errorLogService: ErrorLoggService)
{
        //Angular provides a hook for centralized exception
handling.
        //constructor ErrorHandler(): ErrorHandler
         super();
```

```
    }

    handleError(error) : void {
        this.errorLogService.logError(error);
    }
}
```

Steps 4 – In the 4th step, we will Import global handler and error handler services in the NgModule and it will look like this.

```
import {ErrorLoggService} from './error-logg.service';
import {GlobalErrorHandler} from './global-error.service';

//AppModule class with @NgModule decorator
@NgModule({
  //declarations is used for configure the selectors
  declarations: [
    AppComponent,
  ],
  //Composability and Grouping
  imports: [
    BrowserModule,
    HttpClientModule
  ],
  //Runtime or injector configuration
  //Register global error log service and error handler
  providers: [ErrorLoggService, GlobalErrorHandler],
  //bootstrapped entry component
  bootstrap: [AppComponent]
})
export class AppModule { }
```

Steps 5 – Finally, we got a custom error handler for log error in your application errors.

8.9 What Happens If the Request fails on the Server Due to Poor Network Connection?

HttpClient will return an error instead of a successful response.

Chapter 9
Angular Services

9.1 What Is Angular Service?

Services are commonly used for storing data and making HTTP calls.

The main idea behind a service is to provide an easy way to share the data between the components, and with the help of dependency injection (DI) you can control how the service instances are shared.

Services use to fetch the data from the RESTful API.

9.2 How to Setup and Create services?

Before starting to create a service, you just need to set up a dev environment.

Install **Node.js and npm** if they are not already on your machine.

Then install the **Angular CLI globally**.

```
npm install -g @angular/cli
```

Angular CLI tool will allow you to easily and quickly generate services, components, pipes, and many more files for your project.

Now, create a new project by using the CLI command -

```
ng new MyProject
```

And go to your created project directory and launch the server.

```
ng serve —open
```

Now come to service - execute below the command for generating service class.

```
ng g service MyService
```

It will create the two files in the folder - src/app/

1. my-service.service.spec.ts
2. my-service.service.ts

Now, import my service file into the angular module - app.module.ts file. It will look like this.

```
import { AppComponent } from './app.component';
import {MyService}   from './my-service.service';//Import
Service

//AppModule class with @NgModule decorator
@NgModule({
  //Static, This is the compiler configuration
  //declarations is used for configure the selectors.
  declarations: [
    AppComponent
  ],
  //Composability and Grouping
  //imports used for composing NgModules together.
  imports: [
    BrowserModule
  ],
  //Runtime or injector configuration
  //providers is used for runtime injector configuration.
  providers: [MyService],
  //bootstrapped entry component
  bootstrap: [AppComponent]
})
export class AppModule { }
```

And let's see the created service class -my-service.service.ts

```
import { Injectable } from '@angular/core';

@Injectable()
export class MyService {

  constructor() { }
}
```

Now, you need to create service methods to get, post, put, and delete the users.

```
import { Injectable } from '@angular/core';

@Injectable()
export class MyService {
  constructor() { }

  //I'm using the static data
```

```
  //You can also fetch the data using HttpClient service for
backend APIs.
  users = [
     { "id": 1, "name": "Anil Singh", 'age' :32 },
     { "id": 2, "name": "Aradhya" , 'age' :32},
     { "id": 3, "name": "Reena Singh" , 'age' :32}
  ]

  /* (method) MyService.getUsers(): {
    "id": number;
    "name": string;
    'age': number;
    }[] */
  getUsers(){
    return this.users;
  }
}
```

Now, use this service in the user component for display on UI - my-user.component.ts

```
import { Component, OnInit } from '@angular/core';
import {MyService} from '../my-service.service';

@Component({
  selector: 'app-my-user',
  templateUrl: './my-user.component.html',
  styleUrls: ['./my-user.component.css']
})
export class MyUserComponent implements OnInit {
  userList =[];

  constructor(private service :MyService) {
    //Get the user list by using the my service.
    this.userList = service.getUsers();
  }

  ngOnInit() { }
}
```

And my-user.component.html

```
<h4>User List -</h4>
<table border="1">
  <tr>
    <th>ID</th><th>Name</th><th>Age</th>
  </tr>
  <tr *ngFor="let user of userList">
        <td>{{user.id}}</td><td>{{user.name}}</
td><td>{{user.Age}}</td>
  </tr>
</table>
```

Finally, you got the user list on your components HTML.

9.3 What Is Singleton Service?

In Angular, two ways to make a singleton service:

1. Include the service in the AppModule.
2. Declare that the service should be provided in the application root.

The preferred way to create a singleton service - Form beginning to Angular 6 is:

```
import { Injectable } from '@angular/core';

@Injectable({
  providedIn: 'root',
})
export class CustomerService {
}
```

Another way to create a singleton service - Include service in the AppModule - customer.service.ts

```
import { Injectable } from '@angular/core';

@Injectable()
export class CustomersService {

  constructor() { }
}
```

And app.module.ts -

```
import {CustomerService} from './customers.service';

//AppModule class with @NgModule decorator
@NgModule({
  //Static, this is the compiler configuration
  //declarations is used for configure the selectors.
  declarations: [
    AppComponent
  ],
  //Composability and Grouping
  //imports used for composing NgModules together.
  imports: [
    BrowserModule
  ],
  //Runtime or injector configuration
  //providers is used for runtime injector configuration.
  providers: [CustomerService],
  //bootstrapped entry component
  bootstrap: [AppComponent]
})
export class AppModule { }
```

Chapter 10
Routing and Navigation

10.1 What is Angular Router?

An Angular Router is a tool, library that configures navigations between states and views within your Angular app.

The Routing library is written and maintained by the Angular Core Team.

Angular router has own library package - @angular/router.

```
import {Routes, RouterModule,}  from '@angular/router';
```

The basic concept of Angular Router, allows you to:

1. Redirect a URL to another URL.
2. Resolve data before a page is displayed.
3. Run scripts when a page is activated or deactivated.
4. Lazy load parts of our application.

The router supports both styles with two LocationStrategy providers:

1. **PathLocationStrategy**— this is the default style.
2. **HashLocationStrategy**— adds the route path to the hash (#) in the browser's URL.

10.2 What is Router module?

The Router module is a module that provides the necessary service providers and directives for navigating one view to other in the application.

10.3 What is Routes?

Angular Route is an array of route configurations. The "RouterModule.forRoot" method in the module imports to configure the router.

```
type Routes = Route[];
```

Each Route has the following properties:

```
interface Route {
  path?: string
  pathMatch?: string
  matcher?: UrlMatcher
  component?: Type<any>
  redirectTo?: string
```

```
    outlet?: string
    canActivate?: any[]
    canActivateChild?: any[]
    canDeactivate?: any[]
    canLoad?: any[]
    data?: Data
    resolve?: ResolveData
    children?: Routes
    loadChildren?: LoadChildren
    runGuardsAndResolvers?: RunGuardsAndResolvers
}
```

List of properties and it has the following order:

1. **path:** It uses the route matcher DSL.
2. **pathMatch:** It uses to specifies the matching strategy.
3. **matcher:** It uses to defines a custom strategy for path matching.
4. **component:** It is a component type.
5. **redirectTo:** It is the URL fragment and it will replace the current matched segment.
6. **outlet:** It is the name of the outlet the component.
7. **canActivate:** It is an array of DI tokens and used to handle the CanActivate handlers.
8. **canActivateChild:** It is an array of DI tokens and used to handle the CanActivateChild handlers.
9. **canDeactivate:** It is an array of DI tokens and used to handle the CanDeactivate handlers.
10. **canLoad:** It is an array of DI tokens and used to handle the CanLoad handlers.
11. **data:** It is additional data provided to the component by using the ActivatedRoute.
12. **resolve:** It is a map of DI tokens used to look up data resolvers.
13. **runGuardsAndResolvers:** It is defined when guards and resolvers will be run and by default, they run only when the matrix parameters of the route change.
14. **children:** it is an array of child route definitions.
15. **loadChildren:** It is a reference to lazily loaded child routes.

The following example will help you to understand the Router, Router module, and Routes.

In this example, the array of appRoots describes how to navigate from one view to other views and pass it into RouterModule.forRoot method to configure the router.

```
import { BrowserModule } from '@angular/platform-browser';
import { NgModule } from '@angular/core';
import {Routes, RouterModule,} from '@angular/router';

//Import Components
import { AppComponent } from './app.component';
import { DashboardComponent } from './dashboard/
dashboard.component';
import { UserComponent } from './user/user.component';
import { UserDetailComponent } from './user-detail/user-
detail.component';
import { PageNotFoundComponent } from './page-not-found/
page-not-found.component'

//Apps roots
const appRoots = [
  { path: '', redirectTo: '/dashboard', pathMatch: 'full' },
  { path: 'user/:id', component: UserDetailComponent }, //Id
is a Roots parameter.
    { path: 'users', component: UserComponent, data:{
title:'User List'} },
  { path: '**', redirectTo: 'PageNotFoundComponent' } //Wild
Cards (**), the router will instantiate the PageNotFound
component
];

//AppModule class with @NgModule decorator
@NgModule({
  //Static, this is the compiler configuration
  //declarations is used for configure the selectors
  declarations: [
    AppComponent,
    DashboardComponent,
    UserComponent,
    UserDetailComponent,
    PageNotFoundComponent,
  ],
  //Composability and Grouping
  //imports used for composing NgModules together
  imports: [
    BrowserModule,
```

```
    //enableTracing is used for debugging purposes only
    RouterModule.forRoot(appRoots, { enableTracing: true })
  ],
  //Runtime or injector configuration
  //providers is used for runtime injector configuration
  providers: [],
  //bootstrapped entry component
  bootstrap: [AppComponent]
})
export class AppModule { }
```

10.4 How Angular Router Works?

Angular Router performs the following:

1. The router reads the browser URL that user wants to navigate to.
2. The router applies a URL redirect (if one is defined otherwise page not found the error).
3. It figures out which router state corresponds to the URL.
4. It runs the guards that are defined in the router state.
5. It resolves the required data for the router state.
6. It activates the Angular components to display the page.
7. It manages navigations and repeats the steps above when a new page is requested.

Angular Router introduces the following terms and concepts:

1. <base href>
2. Router imports
3. Configuration
4. Router outlet
5. Router links
6. Router state
7. Activated route
8. Router events

10.5 What Is <base href>?

Most of all Angular routing apps must have the <base> element to the index.html or layout page in the <head> tag.

When using the PathLocationStrategy, need to tell the browsers what will be prefixed to the requested path to generate the URL.

You can specify a base URL like this:

```
  <base href="/">
```

OR

```
<!doctype html>
<html lang="en">
<head>
  <meta charset="utf-8">
  <title>My Demo Apps</title>
  <base href="/">

  <meta name="viewport" content="width=device-width, initial-scale=1">
  <link rel="icon" type="image/x-icon" href="favicon.ico">
</head>
<body>
  <app-root></app-root>
</body>
</html>
```

So if you had an Angular route defined like this –

```
{ path: 'users', component: UserComponent, data:{ title:'User List'} }
```

If <base href="/" >, the route become "/users".

If <base href="/angular" >, the route become "/angular/users".

10.6 How to Append Base URL to HTTP requests?

We can append base URL to HTTP requests using:

1. Dependency Injection
2. Using HttpInterceptors

The following example for append base URL by using DI:

Firstly, we register a base URL provider in the NgModule and after register this BASE_URL, it is available universally in your Apps.

```
  //Runtime or injector configuration
  //providers is used for runtime injector configuration.
  providers: [{ provide: 'BASE_URL', useFactory: getBaseUrl }],
```

Now, provide factory method which gets the base URL from <base> element.

```
export function getBaseUrl() {
  return document.getElementsByTagName('base')[0].href;
}
```

Finally, we can get the base URL injected and add it to URL-

```
export class GetUserComponent {

   constructor(http: Http, @Inject('BASE_URL') baseUrl:
string) {
      http.get(baseUrl + 'api/users').subscribe(data => {
          this.users = data.json();
      }, error => console.error(error));
  }
}
```

The following example for append base URL by using HttpInterceptors:

If we wants to create an interceptor, we must create an Injectable class which implements HttpInterceptor.

Firstly, register interceptor in the module provider:

```
  //Runtime or injector configuration
  //providers is used for runtime injector configuration.
   providers: [{ provide: HTTP_INTERCEPTORS, useClass:
ApiInterceptor, multi: true } ],
```

And after register interceptor:

```
@Injectable()
export class ApiInterceptor implements HttpInterceptor {
   //Intercepts HttpRequest and handles them.
     intercept(req: HttpRequest<any>, next: HttpHandler):
Observable<HttpEvent<any>> {

                                  const baseUrl =
document.getElementsByTagName('base')[0].href;
      const apiReq = req.clone({ url: `${baseUrl}${req.url}`
});
        return next.handle(apiReq);
    }
}
```

Now we can access the base URL across apps.

10.7 What Is PathLocationStrategy?

A LocationStrategy is used to configure the Location service that represents its state in the path of the browser's URL and the PathLocationStrategy is a default routing strategy.

While using the PathLocationStrategy, we must provide *APP_BASE_HREF* in the module or base element in the app document.

10.8 What Is HashLocationStrategy?

To enable HashLocationStrategy in an Angular app {useHash: true}, you must provide routes with router module.

Example:

```
  //Composability and Grouping
  //imports used for composing modules together.
  imports: [
    BrowserModule,
    //enableTracing enables debugging purposes only
     //useHash enables the location strategy that uses the
URL fragment instead of the history API.
     RouterModule.forRoot(appRoots, { enableTracing: true,
useHash:true })
  ],
```

The HashLocationStrategy add the route path to the hash (#) in the browser's URL.

The hash (#) part of the URL is called the hash fragment.

When using HashLocationStrategy for routing and providing a base Href, it is always placed after the hash (#) e.g.

`http://localhost:8080/#/UserDetail/1`

The Hash style routing using the anchor tags technique is used to achieve client side routing and URL never sent to the server.

The anchor tag, when used along with the hash (#) allows us to jump to a place, within apps.

The URL would look like this:

1. http://localhost:8080.
2. http://localhost:8080/#/Users.
3. http://localhost:8080/#/UserDetail/1.

In the above URLs "#/Users" and "#/UserDetail/1" never sent to the server.

10.9 How do you change the base URL Dynamically?

Instead of setting the base element's href value, you can set the base URL programmatically, by providing for APP_BASE_HREF with your custom operation.

10.10 What Is Router Imports?

It is an optional service that presents a special component view for a given URL. It has own library package- @angular/router and It is not a part of an Angular core.

The Angular package will looks like this:

```
import {Routes, RouterModule,}  from '@angular/router';
```

10.11 How to Configure Angular Routes?

A router has no routes until you configure it. So you are configuring the Angular router for accessing your apps URLs.

```
  //Composability and Grouping
  //imports used for composing NgModules together.
  imports: [
    BrowserModule,
    //enableTracing is used for debugging purposes only
   //Enables the location strategy that uses the URL fragment
instead of the history API.
     RouterModule.forRoot(appRoots, { enableTracing: true,
useHash:false })
  ]
```

10.12 What Is Router Outlet?

The Router-Link, RouterLink-Active and the Router outlet is directive provided by the Angular RouterModule package.

It also provides the navigation and URLs manipulation capabilities. It also renders the components for specific location of your applications.

Both the template and templateUrl render the components where you use this directive.

```
<router-outlet> </router-outlet>
```

10.13 Is it possible to have a multiple router-outlet in the same template?

Yes, why not! We can use multiple router-outlets in the same template by configuring our routers and simply adds the router-outlet name.

```
<div class="row">
  <div class="user">
    <router-outlet name="users"></router-outlet>
  </div>
  <div class="detail">
    <router-outlet name="userDetail"></router-outlet>
  </div>
</div>
```

Setups your route config and it will look like this.

```
//Apps roots
const appRoots = [
  { path: '', redirectTo: '/dashboard', pathMatch: 'full' },
  { path: 'userDetail', component: UserDetailComponent }, /
/Id is a Roots parameter.
   { path: 'users', component: UserComponent, data:{
title:'User List'} },
  { path: '**', redirectTo: 'PageNotFoundComponent' } //Wild
Cards, the router will instantiate the PageNotFound component.
];
```

And

```
//AppModule class with @NgModule decorator
@NgModule({
  //Composability and Grouping
  //imports used for composing NgModules together
  imports: [
    BrowserModule,
    //enableTracing is used for debugging purposes only
   //Enables the location strategy that uses the URL fragment
instead of the history API.
    RouterModule.forRoot(appRoots)
  ],
  //bootstrapped entry component
  bootstrap: [AppComponent]
})
export class AppModule { }
```

10.14 What Is Router Link?

The Router-link is a directive and it is used to link a specific part of your applications.

```
@Directive({ selector: ':not(a)[routerLink]' })
```

Let explain the route configuration by using:

```
{ path: 'user/:id', component: UserDetailComponent
```

In the above router configuration, when linking to this user/:id route, you use the RouterLink directive.

If the link is static, you can use the directive:

```
<a routerLink="/user/id"> See the User detail</a>
```

If you use dynamic values to generate the router link than you can pass an array of path segments.

You can specify a route parameter:

```
<a [routerLink]="['/user', user.id]">
  <span class="text-align">{{ user.id }}</span>{{ user.name
}}
</a>
```

You can set query params and fragment as follows:

```
<a [routerLink]="['/user/id']" preserveQueryParams
preserveFragment>
  See the user component
</a>
```

You can specify optional route parameters like this.

```
<a [routerLink]="['/user-detail', { id: '102348014' }]">User
Detail</a>
```

And

```
@Component({
  selector: 'app-user',
  template: '<nav>
    <a [routerLink]="['/users']">User List</a>
    <a [routerLink]="['/userDetail/101', { Id: '102348014'
}]">User Detail</a>
  </nav>
  <router-outlet></router-outlet>',
  styleUrls: ['./user.component.css']
})
```

10.15 What Is RouterLinkActive?

The RouterLinkActive is a directive. To add the active CSS class to the element when the associated RouterLink becomes active.

```
@Directive({
  selector: '[routerLinkActive]',
  exportAs: 'routerLinkActive'
})
```

Consider the following example for active a link:

```
<a routerLink="/user/detail" routerLinkActive="active-
link">User Detail</a>
```

You can also set more than one class and it will look like this.

```
<a routerLink="/user/detail" routerLinkActive="active-class1
active-class2">User detail</a>
<a routerLink="/user/detail" [routerLinkActive]="['active-
class1', 'active-class2']">User detail</a>
```

10.16 What Is RouterState?

RouterState is an interface and it represents the state of the router.

It will look like this:

```
interface RouterState extends Tree {
  snapshot: RouterStateSnapshot
  toString(): string
}
```

It is also a tree of activated routes.

We can access the current RouterState from anywhere in the Angular app by using the Router service and the routerState property.

10.17 What Is ActivatedRoute?

ActivatedRoute is an interface and it contains the information about a route associated with a component loaded into an outlet and it can also be used to traverse the router state tree.

And it contains the list of Properties:

1. **Snapshot:** It is the current snapshot of this route.
2. **URL:** It is an observable of the URL segments and it matched by this route.
3. **Params:** It is an observable of the matrix parameters scoped to this route.
4. **QueryParams:** It is an observable of the query parameters shared by all the routes.
5. **Fragment:** It is an observable of the URL fragment shared by all the routes.
6. **Data:** It is an observable of the static and resolved data of this route.
7. **Outlet;** It's a constant and outlet name of the route.
8. **Component:** It's a constant and a component of the route.
9. **RouteConfig:** This configuration is used to match this route.
10. **Root:** This is the root of the router state.
11. **Parent;** The parent of this route in the router state tree.
12. **FirstChild;** The first child of this route is in the router state tree.
13. **Children;** The children of this route are in the router state tree.
14. **pathFromRoot:** The path from the root of the router state tree to this route.

15. **paramMap:** It is read-only.
16. **queryParamMap:** It is read-only.

10.18 What Is Router Events?

Whenever the root navigations, the router emits navigation events by using Router.events property.

The sequence of router events is:

1. NavigationStart
2. RouteConfigLoadStart
3. RouteConfigLoadEnd
4. RoutesRecognized
5. GuardsCheckStart
6. ChildActivationStart
7. ActivationStart
8. GuardsCheckEnd
9. ResolveStart
10. ResolveEnd
11. ActivationEnd
12. ChildActivationEnd
13. NavigationEnd
14. NavigationCancel
15. NavigationError

The Router events are also logged in the console when enableTracing option is enabled.

The NavigationStart event is triggered when navigation starts.

The RoutesRecognized event triggered when the routes are recognized.

The RouteConfigLoadStart event triggered before the Router lazy loads.

The RouteConfigLoadEnd event triggered after a route has been lazily loaded.

The NavigationEnd event triggered when navigation ends successfully.

The NavigationCancel event triggered when navigation is cancelled.

The NavigationError event triggered when router navigation fails due to an error.

Chapter 11
Angular Compiler

11.1 What Is the Angular Compiler?

The **Angular** compiler converts our **applications code** (HTML and TypeScript) into **JavaScript** code before browser downloads and runs that code.

The **@NgModule** metadata plays an important role in guiding the compilation process and also tells the compiler what components to compile for this module and how to link this module with other modules.

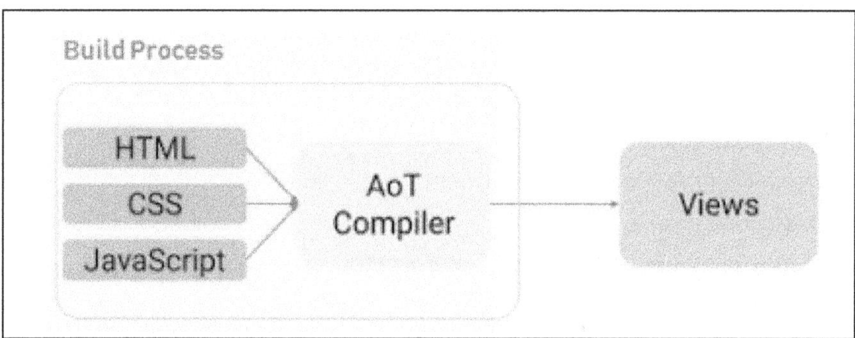

The Angular offers two ways to compile our application code:

1. **Just-in-Time** (**JIT**) - JIT compiles our app in the browser at runtime (compiles before running).
2. **Ahead-of-Time** (**AOT**) - AOT compiles our app at build-time (compiles while running).

The **JIT** compilation is the default when we run the **build** or **serve** CLI commands:

```
ng build
ng serve
```

The **AOT** compilation, we append the **—aot** flags to **build** or **serve** CLI commands:

```
ng build —aot
ng serve —aot
```

11.2 Why we need Compilation in Angular?

We need compilation for achieving a higher level of efficiency, performance improvements, faster rendering and sometimes detect template errors.

11.3 Why Compile with AOT?

1. Faster Rendering
2. Asynchronous Requests
3. Detect template errors earlier
4. Smaller Angular frameworks download size
5. Better Security

11.4 What Is the difference between JIT compiler and AOT compiler?

JIT (Just-in-Time) -

1. JIT compiles our app in the browser at runtime.
2. Compiles before running.
3. Each file compiled separately.
4. No need to build after changing our app code and it automatically reflects the changes in your browser page.
5. Highly secure.
6. Very suitable for local development.

AOT (Ahead-of-Time) -

1. AOT compiles our app code at build time.
2. Compiles while running.
3. Compiled by the machine itself, via the command line (Faster).
4. All code compiled together, in lining HTML/CSS in the scripts.
5. Highly secure.
6. Very suitable for production builds.

Angular Compiler Class :

```
class Compiler {
  // Compiles the given NgModule and all of its components
     compileModuleSync<T>(moduleType:  Type<T>):
NgModuleFactory<T>

  //Compiles the given NgModule and all of its components
    compileModuleAsync<T>(moduleType:  Type<T>):
Promise<NgModuleFactory<T>>

  //creates ComponentFactories for all components
 compileModuleAndAllComponentsSync<T>(moduleType: Type<T>):
ModuleWithComponentFactories<T>

  ////creates ComponentFactories for all components
```

```
    compileModuleAndAllComponentsAsync<T>(moduleType:
Type<T>):Promise<ModuleWithComponentFactories<T>>

  //Clears all caches.
  clearCache(): void

  //Clears the cache for the given component/ngModule.
  clearCacheFor(type: Type<any>)
}
```

11.5 What Is Angular Compiler Options?

We can control app compilations by using the compilerOptions in *tsconfig.json* file.

The tsconfig.json file will look like this:

```
{
  "compileOnSave": false,
  "compilerOptions": {
    "outDir": "./dist/out-tsc",
    "sourceMap": true,
    "declaration": false,
    "moduleResolution": "node",
    "emitDecoratorMetadata": true,
    "experimentalDecorators": true,
    "target": "es5",
    "typeRoots": [
      "node_modules/@types"
    ],
    "lib": [
      "es2017",
      "dom"
    ]
  }
}
```

11.6 What Is Ivy Renderer?

The new Ivy renders and it's not stable for now and it's only in beta version.

Ivy Renderer is new rendering engine which is designed to be backward compatible with existing render and focused to improve the speed of rendering and it optimizes the size of the final package.

The main goal of Ivy render is to speed up its loading time and reduce the bundle size of your applications.

Features of New Ivy engine in Angular 6:

1. Smaller builds.
2. Faster rebuild times.
3. Faster development.
4. A simpler, more hack-able pipeline.
5. Human readable code.

11.7 What Is Bazel Compiler? What Angular is doing with Bazel Compiler?

The Bazel Complier is build-in system used nearly for all software built at Google.

From Angular 6 release, will start having the Bazel compiler support and when you compile the code with Bazel Compiler, you will recompile the entire code base, but it compiles only with necessary code.

The Bazel Complier uses advanced local and distributed caching, optimized dependency analysis and parallel execution.

Bazel allows us to break an application into distinct build units. In Angular, build units are defined at the NgModule level.

This means the scope of a build can be as granular as a single NgModule. If a change is internal to an NgModule, only that module needs to be re-built.

Angular, Angular Universal, NgRx, and Tsickle all switched to Bazel as the build tool, and ship Bazel-built artefacts to npm.

Chapter 12
Angular Pipes

12.1 What Is Pipe?

Pipes transform displayed values within a template.

Use the @Pipe annotation to declare that a given class is a pipe. A pipe class must also implement a PipeTransform interface.

The @Pipe decorator allows you to define the pipe name that is globally available for use in any template across Angular apps.

Pipe class implements the "PipeTransform" interfaces transform method that accepts an input value and returns the transformed result.

There will be one additional argument to the transform method for each parameter passed to the pipe.

The CLI commons to generate Pipe:

```
ng g pipe PipeName
//OR
ng generate pipe PipeName
```

Pipe decorator and metadata:

```
@Pipe({
  name: string
  pure?: boolean
})
```

The pipe name is used for template bindings.

To use the pipe you must set a reference to this pipe class in the module.

12.2 Why use Pipes?

Sometimes, the data is not displayed in the well format on the HTML templates.

You can execute a function in the HTML template to get its returned value.

For example - If you want to display a credit card number on your web apps - you can't display the whole number on your web app - you should write a custom logic to display card number as like ****-****-2485 by using your custom pipe.

12.3 What Is PipeTransform interface?

The Pipe class implements the PipeTransform interface that accepts input value (It is optional parameters) and returns the transformed value.

The transform method is an important method to a pipe.

To create a Pipe, you must implement this interface.

Angular invokes the transform method with the value of a binding as the first, and second argument in list form.

The PipeTransform interface will look like:

```
export interface PipeTransform {
    transform(value: any, ...args: any[]): any;
}
```

And it is imported from Angular core:

```
import {Pipe, PipeTransform} from '@angular/core';
```

Two Categories of Pipes in Angular:

1. pure
2. impure

Every pipe has been pure by default. If you want to make a pipe impure that time you will allow the setting pure flag to false.

12.3.1 What Is Impure Pipe?

Angular executes an impure pipe during every component change detection cycle. An impure pipe is called often, as every keystroke or mouse-move.

If you want to make a pipe impure that time you will allow the setting pure flag to false.

```
@Pipe({
  name: 'currency',
  pure:false
})
```

The example for impure pipe:

```
import { Pipe, PipeTransform } from '@angular/core';

@Pipe({
  name: 'currency',
  pure:false
})
export class CurrencyPipe implements PipeTransform {
```

```
  transform(value: any, args?: any): any {
    if (!value) {
      return '1.00';
    }

    return value;
  }
}
```

12.3.2 What Is Pure Pipe?

Angular executes a pure pipe only when it detects a pure change to the input value. A pure change can be primitive or non-primitive.

Primitive data are single values, they have not special capabilities and the non-primitive data types are used to store the group of values.

```
@Pipe({
  name: 'currency'
})
```

OR

```
@Pipe({
  name: 'currency',
  pure: true
})
```

Another example for a pure pipe:

```
import { Pipe, PipeTransform } from '@angular/core';

@Pipe({
  name: 'currency'
})
export class CurrencyPipe implements PipeTransform {

  transform(value: any, args?: any): any {
    if (!value) {
      return '1.00';
    }

    return value;
  }
}
```

The Pipe operator (|)

The pipe operator is used to specify a value transformation in HTML template or view.

12.4 What Is Parameterizing Pipe?

A pipe can accept any number of optional parameters to achieve output. The parameter value can be any valid template expressions. To add optional parameters follow the pipe name with a colon (:). Its looks like- *currency: 'INR'*

Consider the following example:

```
<h2>The birthday is - {{ birthday | date:"MM/dd/yy" }} </h2>
<!– Output - The birthday is - 10/03/1984 –>
```

12.5 What Is Chaining Pipe?

The chaining Pipe is used to perform the multiple operations within the single expression. This chaining operation will be chained by using the pipe (I).

In the following example, to display the birthday in the upper case- we need to use the inbuilt date-pipe and upper-case-pipe.

Consider the following example –

```
{{ birthday | date | uppercase}}
<!– The output is - MONDAY, MARCH 10, 1984 –>
```

12.6 What Are Inbuilt Pipes in Angular?

Angular defines various Pipes API lists – That is called Inbuilt Pipes.

1. DatePipe
2. CurrencyPipe
3. AsyncPipe
4. DecimalPipe
5. PercentPipe
6. UpperCasePipe
7. LowerCasePipe
8. TitleCasePipe
9. JsonPipe
10. SlicePipe
11. I18nSelectPipe
12. And many more

Similarly, you can also create a custom pipe (as per your needs) and configure in a module that is globally available across angular apps.

12.7 What Is DatePipe?

The DatePipe is used to format a date with the help of locale rules.

```
{{ value_expression | date [ : format [ : timezone [ : locale
] ] ] }}
```

The Example for date pipe:

The full date provides you full date for the date. The short date converts the date to a short date and the long date provides you long date for the date.

```
<h3>{{TodayDate}}</h3>
<h3>{{TodayDate | date:'shortDate'}}</h3>
<h3>{{TodayDate | date:'longDate'}}</h3>
<h3>{{TodayDate | date:'fullDate'}}</h3>
```

12.8 What Is CurrencyPipe?

The CurrencyPipe is used to format a currency with help of locale rules.

```
{{ value_expression | currency [ : currencyCode [ : display
[ : digitsInfo [ : locale ] ] ] ] }}
```

The CurrencyPipe formats a number as a currency of a specific country. It takes country currency type as a parameter.

The example for the currency pipe:

```
<tr>
  <td>{{employee.salary | currency}}</td>
  <td>{{employee.salary | currency : 'INR'}}</td>
 <td>{{employee.salary | currency : 'INR' : true : '6.2'}}</
td>
</tr>
```

12.9 What Is AsyncPipe?

Angular provide a special kind of pipe that are called AsyncPipe and the AsyncPipe subscribes to an observable and returns the latest value it has emitted.

The AsyncPipe allows you to bind your HTML templates directly to values that arrive in an asynchronous manner that has a great ability for the promises and observables.

The expression with Async pipe:

```
{{ obj_expression | async }}
```

OR

```
<ul><li *ngFor="let account of accounts | async">{{account.ACNo
}}</li></ul>
```

The object expression can be observable, promise, null, or undefined.

The example for AsyncPipe:

```
@Component({
  selector: 'app-async-pipe',
 template:'<ul><li *ngFor="let account of accounts | async">
A/C No- {{account.ACNo }} </li></ul>',
  styleUrls: ['./async-pipe.component.css']
})
export class AsyncPipeComponent implements OnInit {
accounts = [];//accounts declarations
apiURL: string = 'https://api.github.com/anilsingh/accounts/
'; //fetching json data from Rest API

//AsyncPipe Component constructor
constructor(private accountService: AccountService) { }

//Load the account list
ngOnInit() {
    this.accountService.getAccount(this.apiURL)
                        .subscribe(data => this.accounts =
data);
}
}
```

12.10 What Is PercentPipe?

Angular provides a PercentPipe and it is used to format a number as a percentage according to below rules.

The expression rule with percent:

```
{{ value_expression | percent [ : digitsInfo [ : locale ] ]
}}
```

The input value to be formatted as a percentage and it can be of any type.

The digitsInfo is optional string parameters and by default it is undefined.

The locale is optional string parameters and by default it is undefined.

The example as,

```
<h2>Result- {{marks | percent}}</h2>
<!— output result is - '98%'—>
```

12.11 What Is LowerCasePipe?

Angular provides a LowerCasePipe and it is used to transforms a given text to lowercase.

The expression with lowercase -

```
{{ value_expression | lowercase }}
```

Consider the example:

```
import { Component } from '@angular/core';

@Component({
  selector: 'lowercase-pipe',
  template: '<div>
                    <input    type="text"    #name
(keyup)="changeLowerCase(name.value)">
    <p>LowerCase - <h2>'{{value | lowercase}}'</h2>
  </div>'
})
export class LowerCasePipeComponent {
  value: string;

  changeLowerCase(value: string) {
    this.value = value;
  }
}
```

12.12 What Is UpperCasePipe?

Angular provides an UpperCasePipe and it is used to transforms a given text to uppercase.

The expression with uppercase:

```
{{ value_expression | uppercase }}
```

Consider the example:

```
import { Component } from '@angular/core';

@Component({
  selector: 'uppercase-pipe',
  template: '<div>
                    <input    type="text"    #name
(keyup)="changeUpperCase(name.value)">
```

```
    <p>UpperCase - <h2>'{{value | uppercase}}'</h2>
  </div>'
})
export class UpperCasePipeComponent {
  value: string;

  changeUpperCase(value: string) {
    this.value = value;
  }
}
```

12.13 What Is TitleCasePipe?

The TitleCasePipe is used to converts the text (string type data) in which the first alphabet of each word is capital and the rest will be in the small case letter. The expression with titlecase:

```
{{ value_expression | titlecase }}
```

Consider the example:

```
import { Component } from '@angular/core';

@Component({
  selector: 'titlecase-pipe',
  template: '<div>
                    <input    type="text"    #name
(keyup)="changetitlecase(name.value)">
    <p>titlecase - <h2>'{{value | titlecase}}'</h2>
  </div>'
})
export class titlecasePipeComponent {
  value: string;

  changetitlecase(value: string) {
    this.value = value;
  }
}
```

Chapter 13
Service Workers

13.1 What Is Service Workers?

A Service Worker is a script which runs in the web browsers and manages to the caching for web applications. This script runs in the separates background and doesn't need any user interactions.

They can query a local cache and deliver a cached response if it is available in the cached. This makes more reliable and increases the performance.

A Service Worker is a programmable network proxy and it intercept all outgoing HTTP requests and control how network requests from your page are handled.

The Service Worker is a method that enables applications to take advantage of persistent data in the background processing, including hooks to enable bootstrapping of web applications while offline.

13.2 What Is Service Workers in Angular?

Angular 5+ start using service workers which increase the reliability and performance of the app without needing to code against this.

This is the great advantages of angular and Angular's service worker is designed to:

1. Improve the performance regarding the unreliable network connection.
2. Minimizing the risks of serving out-dated content.
3. It Optimize the end user experience.

The main design goal of Angular's Service Worker:

1. Caching an application.
2. When users refresh applications, they see firstly latest version cached file.
3. The Updates happen in the background process. Do not interrupt other processes.
4. When Updates happens the previous version of the application is served until an update ready to use

Prerequisites to Supports Service Workers:

We must have the following Angular and Angular CLI versions and also our web application must run in a web browser that supports service workers.

1. Angular 5 or later
2. Angular CLI 1.6 or later

13.3 What Is Service Worker Life Cycle?

A service worker has a life cycle that is completely separate from your web apps page.

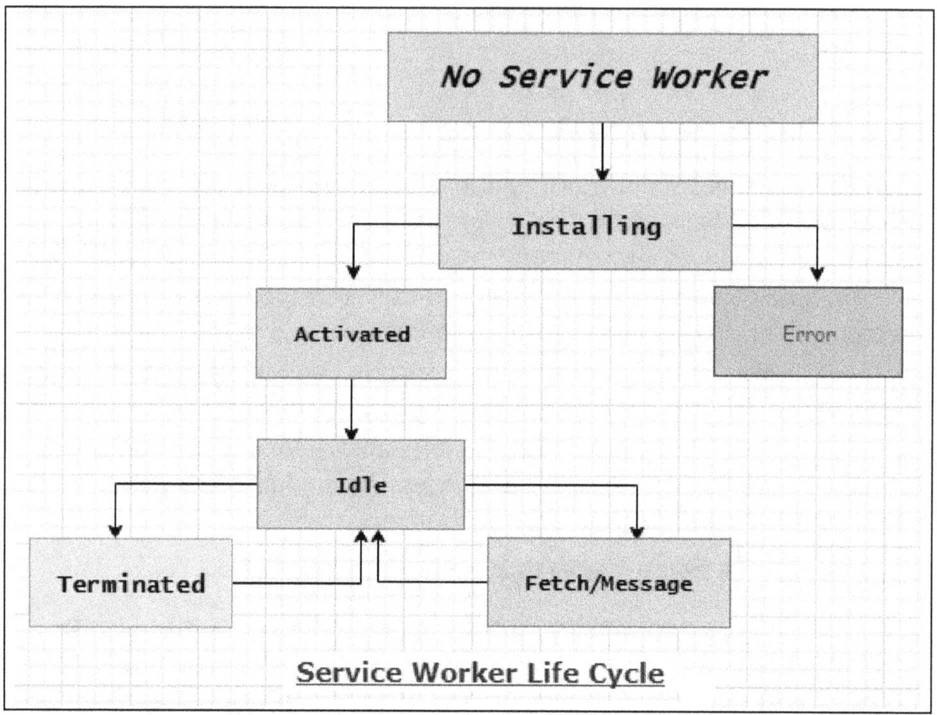

Service Worker Life Cycle

To install a service worker for our site, we need to register it, which we do on our pages. To Register, a service worker will cause the browser to start the service worker install step in the background process.

Prerequisites to Supports Service workers:

1. Browser support
2. You need HTTPS

13.4 How to Register a Service Worker?

To install a service worker you need to kick-start the process by registering it on your page. This tells the browser where your service worker JavaScript file lives.

You can call below register () every time a page loads without concern; the browser will figure out if the service worker is already registered or not and handle it accordingly.

```
if ('serviceWorker' in navigator) {
  window.addEventListener('load', function() {
              navigator.serviceWorker.register('/
sw.js').then(function(registration) {
```

```
      // If Registration was successful
          console.log('Success Registration - ',
registration.scope);
    },
    function(err) {
      // If Registration was failed!
      console.log('Failed Registration - ', err);
    });
  });
}
```

This code checks to see if the service worker API is available, and if it is, the service worker at /sw.js is registered once the page is loaded.

13.5 How to Install a Service Worker?

Consider the following example looks like this.

```
self.addEventListener('install', function(event) {
  // To perform install steps
});
```

Inside of our install callback, we need to follow the following steps:

1. Open a cache.
2. Cache our files.
3. Confirm whether all the required assets are cached or not.

Consider the following example:

```
var CACHE_NAME = 'my-site-cache-v1.0';
var urlsToCache = ['/','/styles/site.css','/script/site.js'];

self.addEventListener('install', function(event) {
  // Perform install steps
  event.waitUntil(
    caches.open(CACHE_NAME)
      .then(function(cache) {
        console.log('Opened cache');
        return cache.addAll(urlsToCache);
      })
  );
});
```

13.6 How to Cache and return Requests?

After a service worker is installed and the user navigates to a different page or refreshes, the service worker will begin to receive fetch events.

Consider the following example:

```
self.addEventListener('fetch', function(event) {
  event.respondWith(
    caches.match(event.request)
      .then(function(response) {
        //Cache return response
        if (response) {
          return response;
        }
        return fetch(event.request);
      })
  );
});
```

13.7 What Is Angular Language Service?

The Language Service is a way to find the typing hints, autocompletion, errors, and navigations inside your templates. It can be an external HTML file or embedded decorators in a string.

Let's understand the following points:

1. **Autocompletion:** It provides you a language hint for speed up the code of your app.
2. **Error checking:** It provides you a warning message on your code mistake.
3. **Navigation:** It allows you to hover to see where a component, directives, modules, and then click or press F12 to go directly to its definition.

Chapter 14

Server Side Rendering (Angular Universal)

14.1 What Is Angular Universal?

Angular Universal is the fastest technology that runs angular apps on the server. It generates static pages of your app on the server via a procedure that is called server-side rendering (SSR). It also generate and serve those pages in response to requests from the browsers.

If you want to make a Universal app, you must install the "platform-server" package.

This package has server implementations of:

1. DOM
2. XMLHttpRequest
3. And other features

The platform-server app doesn't execute in the browsers because you compile the app by using the platform-server module instead of the platform-browser module.

14.2 How to Install Universal?

To get started, you first need to install these packages.

1. @angular/platform-server - It is a universal server-side component and the platform-server app doesn't execute in the browsers.
2. @nguniversal/module-map-ngfactory-loader – It uses for handling lazy-loading in the context of a server-render.
3. @nguniversal/express-engine – It is an express engine for a universal app.
4. ts-loader - To transpile the server application

Also, you can install these packages by using the following command:

npm install —save @angular/platform-server @nguniversal/module-map-ngfactory-loader ts-loader @nguniversal/express-engine

14.3 Why Angular Universal?

There are three main reasons to create a universal app.

1. Improve performance on mobile and other devices.
2. Facilitate web crawlers. The crawling is a SEO part of your app.
3. Render the first page quickly.

Google, Bing, Twitter, Facebook, and other social media sites depend on web crawlers to index your app content and make that content searchable on the web.

14.4 What Is Universal Web Server?

A Universal web server responds to application page requests with static HTML rendered by the Universal template engine.

The Universal template engine will look like:

```
app.engine('html', ngExpressEngine({
  bootstrap: AppServerModuleNgFactory,
  providers: [
    provideModuleMap(LAZY_MODULE_MAP)
  ]
}));
```

The ngExpressEngine function returns a promise that resolves to the rendered page.

The express-engine is a wrapper class around the renderModuleFactory function that turns a client request into the server-rendered HTML pages.

The AppServerModule is a bridge between the server-side renderer and your app.

Chapter 15
Angular Security

15.1 What are the key points to keep in mind when you are developing Angular apps?

There are four key points to keep in mind when you are developing an Angular's apps i.e.

1. The application level securities like authentication and authorization.
2. Coding with Best Practices.
3. Preventing cross-site scripting (XSS).
4. Reporting vulnerabilities and HTTP Level vulnerabilities.

15.2 How to write Best Practices Applications?

As per experts, be careful when developing Angular apps:

1. We keep and watching the latest version of Angular.
2. Don't try to add hacks or modify to Angular generates files.
3. Avoid Angular's Security Risk.
4. Also, avoid direct use of the DOM APIs.
5. Try to use offline template compiler.
6. Try to prevent CSRF or XSRF attacks in your web apps.
7. Try to prevent JSON data in your web apps.

15.3 What Is Cross Site Scripting (XSS) Attack?

The Cross Site Scripting (XSS) attack is a type of injection and attackers inject your web applications by using the client side scripts and malicious code into web pages.

An attacker can insert vulnerability scripts and malicious code in your web applications.

The Cross Site Scripting (XSS) attacks are common on web browsers and it is carried out on websites around 84% (approximately).

15.4 How To Preventing Cross Site Scripting (XSS) in Angular? How Angular Protects Us From XSS Attacks?

The Angular treats all values as untrusted by default. This is the great advantages of Angular.

Value is Inserted Vulnerability into the DOM from:

1. A Template
2. Property
3. Attribute
4. Style
5. Class Binding
6. Interpolation
7. And so on.

Angular recognizes the value as unsafe and automatically sanitizes and removes the **script tag** and other **security** vulnerabilities.

Angular provides built-in, values as untrusted by default, anti XSS, and CSRF/XSRF protection.

The CookieXSRFStrategy class takes care of preventing XSS and CSRF/XSRF attacks.

The DomSanitizationService takes care of removing the dangerous bits in order to prevent XSS attacks.

Angular applications must follow the same security principles as regular web applications:

1. You should avoid direct use of the DOM APIs.
2. You should enable Content Security Policy (CSP) and configure your web server to return appropriate CSP HTTP headers.
3. You should Use the offline template compiler.
4. You should Use Server-Side XSS protection.
5. You should Use DOM Sanitizer.
6. You should Preventing CSRF or XSRF attacks.

Angular defines the following security -

HTML is used when interpreting a value as HTML i.e.

```
<div [innerHTML]="UNTRUSTED"></div>
OR
<input value="UNTRUSTED">
```

Style is used when binding CSS into the style property i.e.

```
<div [style]="height:UNTRUSTED"></div>
```

URL is used for URL properties i.e.

```
<a [href]="UNTRUSTED-URL"></a>
OR
<script [src]="UNTRUSTED-URL"></script>
OR
<iframe src="UNTRUSTED-URL" />
```

Resource URL is a URL that will be loaded and executed i.e.

```
<script>var value='UNTRUSTED';</script>


<p class="e2e-inner-html-interpolated">{{htmlSnippet}}</p>
<p class="e2e-inner-html-bound" [innerHTML]="htmlSnippet"></
p>
```

15.5 Impact of Cross Site Scripting (XSS)

When attackers successfully exploit XSS vulnerabilities in a web application, they can insert scripts and malicious code.

An Attacker can:

1. Hijack user's account.
2. Access browser history and clipboard contents.
3. Application cookies, sessions.
4. Control the browser remotely.
5. Scan and exploit intranet appliances and applications.

Angular defines the following security:

Resource URL is a URL that will be loaded and executed i.e.

```
<script>var value='UNTRUSTED';</script>

<p class="e2e-inner-html-interpolated">{{htmlSnippet}}</p>
<p class="e2e-inner-html-bound" [innerHTML]="htmlSnippet"></
p>
```


Malicious Scripts and Code – Vulnerability

```
<META HTTP-EQUIV="refresh" CONTENT="0; URL=http://
;URL=javascript:alert('XSS');">
<IFRAME SRC="javascript:alert('XSS');"></IFRAME>
<IFRAME SRC=# onmouseover="alert(document.cookie)"></IFRAME>
<TABLE><TD BACKGROUND="javascript:alert('XSS')">
<EMBED SRC="data:image/
svg+xml;base64,PHN2ZyB4bWxuczpzdmc9Imh0dH
A6Ly93d3cudzMub3JnLzIwMDAvc3ZnIiB4bWxucz0iaHR0cDovL3d3dy53My5vcmcv
MjAwMC9zdmciIHhtbG5zOnhsaW5rPSJodHRwOi8vd3d3LnczLm9yZy8xOTk5L3hs
aW5rIiB2ZXJzaW9uPSIxLjAiIHg9IjAiIHk9IjAiIHdpZHRoPSIxOTQiIGhlaWdodD0iMjAw
IiBpZD0ieHNzIj48c2NyaXB0IHR5cGU9InRleHQvZWNtYXNjcmlwdCI+YWxlcnQoIlh
TUyIpOzwvc2NyaXB0Pjwvc3ZnPg=="type="image/svg+xml"
AllowScriptAccess="always"></EMBED>
<SCRIPT>document.write("<SCRI");</SCRIPT>PT SRC="httx://
xss.rocks/xss.js"></SCRIPT>
```

15.6 How does Angular handle with XSS or CSRF? How Angular prevents this attack?

Angular applications must follow the same security principles as regular web applications:

1. You should avoid direct use of the DOM APIs.
2. You should enable Content Security Policy (CSP) and configure your web server to return appropriate CSP HTTP headers.
3. You should Use the offline template compiler.
4. You should Use Server-Side XSS protection.
5. You should Use DOM Sanitizer.
6. You should Preventing CSRF or XSRF attacks.

Example:

```
export const BROWSER_SANITIZATION_PROVIDERS: Array<any> = [
  {provide: Sanitizer, useExisting: DomSanitizer},
  {provide: DomSanitizer, useClass: DomSanitizerImpl},
];

@NgModule({
  providers: [
    BROWSER_SANITIZATION_PROVIDERS
    ...
  ],
  exports: [CommonModule, ApplicationModule]
})
export class BrowserModule {}
```

DOM sanitization - Use to clean untrusted parts of values -

```
export enum SecurityContext { NONE, HTML, STYLE, SCRIPT, URL, RESOURCE_URL }

export abstract class DomSanitizer implements Sanitizer {
   abstract sanitize(context: SecurityContext, value: SafeValue|string|null): string|null;
  abstract bypassSecurityTrustHtml(value: string): SafeHtml;
  abstract bypassSecurityTrustStyle(value: string): SafeStyle;
   abstract bypassSecurityTrustScript(value: string): SafeScript;
  abstract bypassSecurityTrustUrl(value: string): SafeUrl;
   abstract bypassSecurityTrustResourceUrl(value: string): SafeResourceUrl;
}
```

The DOM Sanitize Methods:

```
sanitize(ctx: SecurityContext, value: SafeValue|string|null):
string|null {
  if (value == null) return null;

  switch (ctx) {
    case SecurityContext.NONE:
      return value as string;

    case SecurityContext.HTML:
          if (value instanceof SafeHtmlImpl) return
value.changingThisBreaksApplicationSecurity;
      this.checkNotSafeValue(value, 'HTML');
      return sanitizeHtml(this._doc, String(value));

    case SecurityContext.STYLE:
          if (value instanceof SafeStyleImpl) return
value.changingThisBreaksApplicationSecurity;
      this.checkNotSafeValue(value, 'Style');
      return sanitizeStyle(value as string);

    case SecurityContext.SCRIPT:
          if (value instanceof SafeScriptImpl) return
value.changingThisBreaksApplicationSecurity;
      this.checkNotSafeValue(value, 'Script');
         throw new Error('unsafe value used in a script
context');

    case SecurityContext.URL:
        if (value instanceof SafeResourceUrlImpl || value
instanceof SafeUrlImpl) {
          //Allow resource URLs in URL contexts, they are
strictly more trusted.
        return value.changingThisBreaksApplicationSecurity;
      }
      this.checkNotSafeValue(value, 'URL');
      return sanitizeUrl(String(value));

    case SecurityContext.RESOURCE_URL:
      if (value instanceof SafeResourceUrlImpl) {
        return value.changingThisBreaksApplicationSecurity;
      }
      this.checkNotSafeValue(value, 'ResourceURL');
      throw new Error(
```

```
        'unsafe value used in a resource URL context (see
http://g.co/ng/security#xss)');

    default:
     throw new Error('Unexpected SecurityContext ${ctx} (see
http://g.co/ng/security#xss)');
  }
}
```

15.7 How to Bypass Angular XSS Protection?

Example 1:

```
import {BrowserModule, DomSanitizer} from '@angular/platform-
browser'
```

```
@Component({
  selector: 'my-app',
  template: '<div [innerHtml]="html"></div>',
})
export class App {
  constructor(private sanitizer: DomSanitizer) {
                                    this.html          =
sanitizer.bypassSecurityTrustHtml('<h1>DomSanitizer</
h1><script>alert("XSS")</script>') ;
  }
}
```

Example 2:

```
import {BrowserModule, DomSanitizer} from '@angular/platform-
browser'
```

```
@Component({
  selector: 'my-app',
  template: '<iframe [src]="iframe"></iframe>',
})
export class App {
  constructor(private sanitizer: DomSanitizer) {
                                  this.iframe          =
sanitizer.bypassSecurityTrustResourceUrl("https://www.code-
sample.com")
  }
}
```

15.8 How to Sanitize a Value Manually in Angular?

As per our project requirement, we sanitize a value manually by using the below sanitize methods:

1. SecurityContext.HTML
2. SecurityContext.SCRIPT
3. SecurityContext.STYLE
4. SecurityContext.NONE
5. SecurityContext.RESOURCE_URL
6. SecurityContext.URL

Example 1:

```
import {Component, SecurityContext} from '@angular/core'

export class App {
  constructor(private sanitizer: DomSanitizer) {
      this.html = sanitizer.sanitize(SecurityContext.HTML,
"<h2>DOM Sanitize</h2><script>alert("XSS")</script>");
  }
}
```

Example 2:

```
import {Component, SecurityContext} from '@angular/core'

export class App {
  constructor(private sanitizer: DomSanitizer) {
   this.script = sanitizer.sanitize(SecurityContext.SCRIPT,
"<h2>DOM Sanitize</h2><script>alert("XSS")</script>");
  }
}
```

Example 3:

```
import {Component, SecurityContext} from '@angular/core'

export class App {
  constructor(private sanitizer: DomSanitizer) {
      this.url = sanitizer.sanitize(SecurityContext.URL,
"<h2>DOM Sanitize</h2><script> Your code also");
  }
}
```

15.9 How to Prevent HTML DOM Based XSS attacks?

```
<script type="text/javascript">
  let escapeHTML = function(unsafe_str) {
    return unsafe_str
        .replace(/&/g, '&amp;')
        .replace(/</g, '&lt;')
        .replace(/>/g, '&gt;')
        .replace(/\"/g, '&quot;')
        .replace(/\'/g, '&#39;')
        .replace(/\//g, '&#x2F;')
        .replace('src','drc');
}

//Bind HTML - DOM
element.innerHTML = escapeHTML(iputData);

</script>
```

Chapter 16
Angular Cookies

16.1 What is a Cookie?

A cookie is a small piece of data sent from a website and stored on the user's machine by the user's web browsers while the user is browsing.

OR

Cookies are the small packages of information that are typically stored in your browsers and websites tend to use cookies for multiple things.

16.2 How to install a cookie in Angular?

Install cookie

```
npm install ngx-cookie-service -save
```

If you do not want to install this via NPM, you can run npm run compile and use the *.d.ts and *.js files in the dist-lib folder

After installed successfully, add the cookie service in the Angular module - app.module.ts

```
import {CookieService} from 'ngx-cookie-service'

//AppModule class with @NgModule decorator
@NgModule({
  //Static, this is the compiler configuration
  //declarations is used for configure the selectors.
  declarations: [
    AppComponent
],
  //Composability and Grouping
  //imports used for composing NgModules together.
  imports: [
    BrowserModule
  ],
  //Runtime or injector configuration
  //providers is used for runtime injector configuration.
  providers: [CookieService],
  //bootstrapped entry component
  bootstrap: [AppComponent]
})
export class AppModule { }
```

Then, import and inject it into a component:

```
import { Component, OnInit } from '@angular/core';
import {CookieService} from 'ngx-cookie-service'

@Component({
  selector: 'app-on-click',
  templateUrl: './on-click.component.html',
  styleUrls: ['./on-click.component.css']
})
export class OnClickComponent implements OnInit {

  cookieValue ="";
  constructor(private cookie:CookieService) {   }

  ngOnInit() {
    this.cookie.set('cookie', 'demoApp' );
    this.cookieValue = this.cookie.get('cookie');
  }
}
```

16.3 What are the cookies methods?

Angular cookies concept is very similar to the Angular 1.x but Angular adds only one extra method to delete all cookies.

All cookie methods are:

1. **Check:** This method is used to check the cookie existing or not.
2. **Get:** This method returns the value of given cookie name.
3. **GetAll:** This method returns a value object with all the cookies.
4. **Set:** This method is used to set the cookies with a name.
5. **Delete:** This method is used to delete the cookie with the given name.
6. **deleteAll:** This method is used to delete all the cookies.

16.4 Cookie Methods

The Angular cookies service contains the following methods.

```
export declare class CookieService {
    private document;
    private documentIsAccessible;
    constructor(document: any);
    /**
     * @param name Cookie name
     * @returns {boolean}
```

```
     */
    check(name: string): boolean;
    /**
     * @param name Cookie name
     * @returns {any}
     */
    get(name: string): string;
    /**
     * @returns {}
     */
    getAll(): {};
    /**
     * @param name    Cookie name
     * @param value   Cookie value
    * @param expires Number of days until the cookies expires
or an actual 'Date'
     * @param path    Cookie path
     * @param domain  Cookie domain
     * @param secure  Secure flag
     */
   set(name: string, value: string, expires?: number | Date,
path?: string, domain?: string, secure?: boolean): void;
    /**
     * @param name   Cookie name
     * @param path   Cookie path
     * @param domain Cookie domain
     */
     delete(name: string, path?: string, domain?: string):
void;
    /**
     * @param path   Cookie path
     * @param domain Cookie domain
     */
    deleteAll(path?: string, domain?: string): void;
    /**
     * @param name Cookie name
     * @returns {RegExp}
     */
    private getCookieRegExp(name);
}
```

16.5 How to set in Angular cookies, type number values? Why is Token Based Authentication more preferable Then Cookie based?

The cookie-based authentication has been the default and the cookie-based authentication is stateful.

16.6 What is Stateful?

Keep and track the previously stored information which is used for a current transaction.

A stateful service based on HTTP cookies uses the HTTP transport protocol and its ability to convey cookies, used as session context.

16.7 What are the Cookies Limitations?

We can only store around 20 cookies per web server and not more than 4KB of information in each cookie and they can last indefinitely.

Token Based Authentication

The Token-based authentication has received expansion over last few years due to RESTful Web APIs, SPA and so on.

The Token based authentication is stateless.

16.8 What is Stateless?

Every transaction is performed as if it was being done for the very first time and there is no previously stored information used for the current transaction.

Token Based Authentication steps:

A user enters their login credentials and the server verifies the entered credentials. Validating to the entered credentials, It's correct or not. If the credentials are correct, returns a signed token.

This token is stored in local storage on the client side. We can also store in session storage or cookie.

Advantages of Token-Based Authentication

1. Stateless.
2. Scalable.
3. Decoupled.
4. JWT is placed in the browsers local storage.
5. Protect Cross Domain and CORS.
6. Store Data in the JWT.
7. Protect XSS and XSRF Protection.

16.9 Where to Store Tokens?

It depends on user, where user wants to store the JWT. The JWT is placed in user's browsers local storage.

Chapter 17

Basic Understanding of Angular Testing

17.1 What Is Testing?

The testing is a tools and techniques for a unit and integration testing Angular applications.

17.2 Why Test?

Tests are the best ways to prevent software bugs and defects.

17.3 How to Setup Test in Angular Project?

Angular CLI install everything you need to test an Angular application.

This CLI command takes care of Jasmine and karma configuration for you.

Run this CLI command-

```
ng test
```

The test file extension must be ".spec.ts" so that tooling can identify the test file.

You can also unit test your app by using other testing libraries and test runners.

17.4 Test

All great developer knows his/her testing tools. Understanding your tools for testing is essential before diving into writing tests.

The Testing depends on your project requirements and the project cost. The types of Testing are:

1. Unit Test
2. Integration Test
3. End to End (e2e) Test

What is Unit Test in Angular?

The Unit Test is used to test a single function, single components in Isolation. This is very fast.

The Unit Test is sometimes called as isolated testing

What Is Integration Testing in Angular?

The Integration Testing is used to testing a component with templates and this testing containing more time as per comparison Unit Test.

What is End-to-End (e2e) Testing in Angular?

The End to End Testing is used to test the entire application, such as:

1. All User Interactions.
2. All Service Calls.
3. Authentication/Authorization of app.
4. Everything of App.

e2e testing is done with your actual Services and APIs calls.

Recommended Unit Testing Tools:

1. Karma
2. Jasmine and
3. QUnit

17.5 Do I Need to Use Protractor?

A protractor is an official library to use for writing End-to-End (e2e) test suites with an Angular app. It is nothing but a wrapper over the Selenium WebDriverJS APIs.

If you have been using Angular CLI, you might know that by default, it comes shipped with two frameworks for testing. They are:

1. unit tests by using Jasmine and Karma
2. end-to-end tests by using Protractor

The apparent difference between the two is that the former is used to test the logic of the components and services, while the latter is used to ensure that the high-level functionality of the application works as expected.

Protractor configuration file is - protractor.conf.js and it look like this:

```
//Protractor configuration file
const { SpecReporter } = require('jasmine-spec-reporter');

exports.config = {
  allScriptsTimeout: 11000,
  specs: [
    './e2e/**/*.e2e-spec.ts'
  ],
  capabilities: {
    'browserName': 'chrome'
  },
  directConnect: true,
  baseUrl: 'http://localhost:4200/',
  framework: 'jasmine',
  jasmineNodeOpts: {
    showColors: true,
```

```
    defaultTimeoutInterval: 30000,
    print: function() {}
  },
  onPrepare() {
    require('ts-node').register({
      project: 'e2e/tsconfig.e2e.json'
    });
    jasmine.getEnv().addReporter(new SpecReporter({ spec: {
displayStacktrace: true } }));
  }
};
```

17.6 What Is Test Function?

After installing everything as per your project requirements, CREATE your project. Follow the following Steps:

1 ng new YourTestProject

2 ng install

2 ng serve/ng test

Note – If you are going to develop project then type "ng server" command and if you want to test your project, you should type "ng test" command. After typing "ng test" command, press enter. It will take some time to install everything in your project for a test.

Test functions:

1. describe – Test suit (just a function).
2. it - The spec or test.
3. expect - Expected outcome.

Triple Rule of Testing:

1. Arrange - Create and Initialize the Components.
2. Act - Invoke the Methods/Functions of Components.
3. Assert - Assert the expected outcome/behaviour.

Best Practices - The quick list of best practices.

1. Use beforeEach() to Initialize the context for your tests.
2. Make sure the string descriptions you put in describe () and it () make sense as output.
3. Use after () and afterEach () to clean-up your tests if there is any state that may bleed over.
4. If any one test is over 15 lines of code, you may need to refactor the test

Consider an example:

```
import { TestBed, async } from '@angular/core/testing';
import { AppComponent } from './app.component';

//describe - Test suit (just a function)
describe('AppComponent', () => {
  beforeEach(async(() => {
    TestBed.configureTestingModule({
      declarations: [AppComponent]
    }).compileComponents();
  }));

  //it - The spec or test
  it('should have hello property', function() {
  const fixture = TestBed.createComponent(AppComponent);
  const app = fixture.debugElement.componentInstance;

  //expect - this is expected outcome.
   expect(app.hello).toBe('Hello, Anil!');
 });
});
```

17.7 What is the Jasmine test framework?

Why Jasmine?

Jasmine is a JavaScript testing framework that supports a software development practice called Behaviour Driven Development which plays very well with Karma. It's a specific flavor of Test Driven Development (TDD).

Jasmine is also dependency-free and doesn't require a DOM.

Jasmine provides a rich set of pre-defined matchers - default set of matchers

1. expect(number).toBeGreaterThan(number);
2. expect(number).toBeLessThan(number);
3. expect(array).toContain(member);
4. expect(array).toBeArray();
5. expect(fn).toThrow(string);
6. expect(fn).toThrowError(string);
7. expect(instance).toBe(instance); represents the exact equality (===) operator.
8. expect(mixed).toBeDefined();
9. expect(mixed).toBeFalsy();

10. expect(mixed).toBeNull();
11. expect(mixed).toBeTruthy();
12. expect(mixed).toBeUndefined();
13. expect(mixed).toEqual(mixed); represents the regular equality (==) operator.
14. expect(mixed).toMatch(pattern); calls the RegExp match() method behind the scenes to compare string data.
15. expect(number).toBeCloseTo(number, decimalPlaces);
16. expect(number).toBeNaN();
17. expect(spy).toHaveBeenCalled();
18. expect(spy).toHaveBeenCalledTimes(number);
19. expect(date).toBeAfter(otherDate);
20. expect(date).toBeBefore(otherDate);
21. expect(date).toBeDate();
22. expect(date).toBeValidDate();
23. expect(object).toHaveDate(memberName);
24. expect(object).toHaveDateAfter(memberName, date);
25. expect(object).toHaveDateBefore(memberName, date);
26. expect(regexp).toBeRegExp();
27. expect(string).toBeEmptyString();
28. expect(string).toBeHtmlString();
29. expect(string).toBeIso8601();
30. expect(string).toBeJsonString();
31. expect(string).toBeLongerThan();
32. expect(string).toBeString();

Default set of Asymmetric Matchers-

1. jasmine.any(Constructor);
2. jasmine.anything(mixed);
3. jasmine.arrayContaining(mixed);
4. jasmine.objectContaining(mixed);
5. jasmine.stringMatching(pattern);

Lest see the testing example for AppComponent:

```
import { TestBed, async } from '@angular/core/testing';
import { AppComponent } from './app.component';

describe('AppComponent', () => {
  beforeEach(async(() => {
    TestBed.configureTestingModule({
      declarations: [
        AppComponent
      ],
    }).compileComponents();
  }));

  it('should create the app', async(() => {
    const fixture = TestBed.createComponent(AppComponent);
    const app = fixture.debugElement.componentInstance;

    expect(app).toBeTruthy();
  }));

  it('should have as title 'app'', async(() => {
    const fixture = TestBed.createComponent(AppComponent);
    const app = fixture.debugElement.componentInstance;

    expect(app.title).toEqual('app');
  }));

  it('should render title in a h1 tag', async(() => {
    const fixture = TestBed.createComponent(AppComponent);
    fixture.detectChanges();
    const compiled = fixture.debugElement.nativeElement;

   expect(compiled.querySelector('h1').textContent).toContain('Welcome
to app!');
  }));
});
```

17.8 What Is TestBed?

The Angular TestBed (ATB) is a higher level Angular testing framework that allows you to easily test the behavior that depends on the Angular Framework.

The TestBed creates dynamically and The *TestBed.configureTestingModule*() method takes a metadata object.

We write our tests in Jasmine and run it by using Karma but we now have a slightly easier way to create components, handle injection, test asynchronous behaviour and interact with our application.

Objective questions:

Which of the following can be used to run unit test?

1. Karma
2. Protractor

Answer: Karma!

Which of the following can be used to run end-to-end test?

1. Karma
2. Protractor

Answer: Protractor!

Test doubles are needed while writing which of the following?

1. Unit tests
2. End-to-end tests

Answer: Unit tests!

Which of the following will need Angular testing utilities for unit testing?

1. Services
2. Components
3. All the above

Answer: Components!

It is recommended to write isolated unit tests for which of the following?

1. Services
2. Pipes
3. All the above

Answer: All the above!

Which of the following TestBed method is used to create an Angular component under test?

1. createComponent
2. createTestingComponent
3. configureComponent
4. configureTestingComponent

Answer: createComponent!

Chapter 18
Basic Understanding of TypeScript

18.1 What is TypeScript?

TypeScript is strongly typed, object-oriented, and compiled programming language. This language was developed and maintained by Microsoft.

It was designed by "Anders Hejlsberg" at Microsoft.

It is a superset of JavaScript.

The TypeScript is JavaScript and also has some additional features like static typing and class-based object-oriented programming, automatic assignment of constructor parameters, assigned null values and so on.

The entire JavaScript program is valid for TypeScript because the entire TypeScript (.ts) file is converted to JavaScript (.js) file after source code is compiled and this process is automatic.

18.2 Why should you use TypeScript? What are the Benefits of Using TypeScript?

1. Supports Object Oriented Programming.
2. Typescript adds static typing to JavaScript. Having static typing makes easier to develop and maintain complex apps.
3. Angular2 uses TypeScript a lot to simplify relations between various components and how the framework is built in general.
4. Provide an optional type system for JavaScript.
5. Provide planned features from future JavaScript editions to current JavaScript engines.
6. Supports type definitions.

18.3 What are Types in TypeScript?

The Type represents the different types of values which are using in the programming languages and it checks the validity of the supplied values before they are manipulated by programs.

The TypeScript provides data types as a part of its optional type and also provides us some primitive types as well as a dynamic type "any" and this "any" work like "dynamic".

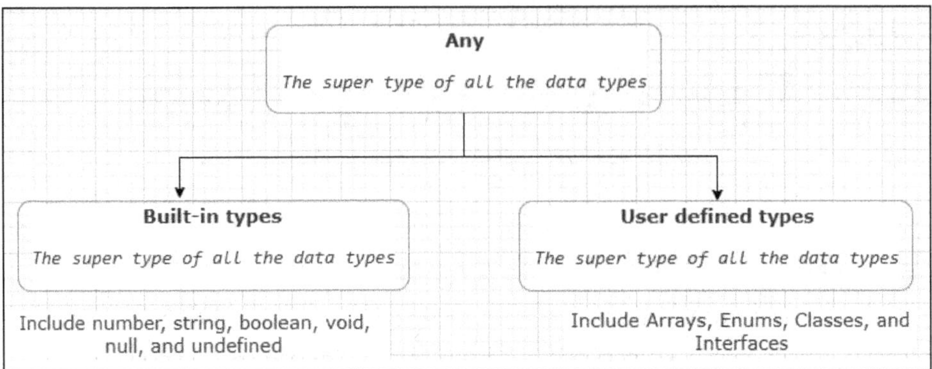

In TypeScript, we define a variable with a "type" and appending the "variable name" with "colon" followed by the type name.

Consider the following example:

```
let isActive: boolean = false; //OR var isActive: boolean = false;
let decimal: number = 6; //OR var decimal: number = 6;
let hex: number = 0xf00d; //OR var hex: number = 0xf00d;
let name: string = "Anil Singh"; //OR var name: string = "Anil Singh";
let binary: number = 0b1010; //OR var binary: number = 0b1010;
let octal: number = 0o744; //OR var octal: number = 0o744;
let numlist: number[] = [1, 2, 3]; //OR var numlist: number[] = [1, 2, 3];
let arrlist: Array<number> = [1, 2, 3]; //OR var arrlist: Array<number> = [1, 2, 3];
```

And

```
//Any Keywords
let list: any[] = [1, true, "free"];
list[1] = 100;
```

And

```
//Any Keywords
let notSureType: any = 10;
notSureType = "maybe a string instead";
notSureType = false; // definitely a Boolean
```

- **Number** - the "number" is a primitive number type in TypeScript. There is a no different type of float or double in TypeScript.
- **Boolean** - The "boolean" type represents true or false condition.

- **String** -The "string" represents a sequence of characters similar to C#.
- **Null** - The "null" is a special type which assigns a null value to a variable.
- **Undefined** - The "undefined" is also a special type of data and can be assigned to any variable.
- **Any** - this data type is the super-type of all types in TypeScript. It is also known as a dynamic type and using "any" type is equivalent to opting out of type checking for a variable.
- **A note about "let" keyword**:

  You may have noticed that the "let" keyword is used instead of "var" keyword. The "let" keyword is actually a newer JavaScript construct that TypeScript makes available.

  Actually, many common problems in JavaScript are reducing by using "let" keyword. So we should use "let" keyword instead of "var" keyword.

www.ingramcontent.com/pod-product-compliance
Lightning Source LLC
LaVergne TN
LVHW022348060326
832902LV00022B/4309

* 9 7 8 9 3 8 8 1 7 6 6 9 9 *